WAKE UP, MRS MOORE

Julie Marie Myatt

BROADWAY PLAY PUBLISHING INC
New York
www.broadwayplaypub.com
info@broadwayplaypub.com

Cover photo by Julie Marie Myatt

First edition: December 2020
I S B N: 978-0-88145-818-3

Book design: Marie Donovan
Page make-up: Adobe InDesign
Typeface: Palatino

WAKE UP, MRS MOORE was commissioned by
Roundabout Theatre Company.

CHARACTERS & SETTING

Virginia Moore
Glenn Moore
Alma Jennings
George Larson
Susan Jones
Tracy Jennings

Time: 1970-2013

Small apartments, Washington, DC, nursing homes, Virginia's *mind.*

Virginia's *mind/coma state:* Virginia's *coma world is dream-driven. It must sound, look, feel, celebrate the Other. Anything is possible. Mixture of dreams and reality; France and fantasy, caught between two worlds.*

Glenn's *apartment (ACT TWO): The antithesis of* Virginia's *dream state. A beige box.*

NOTE ON MUSIC

"The feminine mystique has succeeded in burying millions of American women alive."
Betty Friedan

"Some women choose to follow men, and some women choose to follow their dreams. If you're wondering which way to go, remember that your career will never wake up and tell you that it doesn't love you anymore."
Lady Gaga

ACT ONE

Scene 1

(August 26, 1970. Georgetown, District of Columbia)

(Afternoon sun pours into the humble, one room apartment. Books everywhere)

(An empty bottle of wine.)

(VIRGINIA and GLENN MOORE lie under the covers of the bed, casually singing along with the stereo. Maybe a song like Crosby, Stills, and Nash's, Helplessly Hoping.*)*

(VIRGINIA puts her underwear on under the covers. GLENN takes a sip from a wine glass beside the bed.)

(The song continues as VIRGINIA looks at the watch on GLENN's wrist, and gets up to get dressed.)

(He grabs her leg.)

GLENN: You have to go?

VIRGINIA: Yes.

(VIRGINIA squirms out of GLENN's grip to find her T-shirt. Slips it on)

GLENN: What about dinner?

(VIRGINIA finds a stack of home-made signs on the floor next to her shoes.)

VIRGINIA: Everything's ready in the fridge.

GLENN: Uh huh.

(VIRGINIA *kisses* GLENN.)

VIRGINIA: Just read the recipe.

GLENN: I know—

VIRGINIA: Follow the instructions. You can do it.
(She kisses him again.)

GLENN: Have fun.
(He turns over.)

VIRGINIA: I'm not going there to have fun, you know.

GLENN: Okay.

(VIRGINIA quickly brushes her hair.)

VIRGINIA: It's not a tupperware party.

GLENN: But it is possible. That it could. For one
moment or two. Be fun.

VIRGINIA: Yes. It is possible.
(Silence)
But you never say "have fun" when I protest the war.
Is it because this is a "girl" thing?

(GLENN turns over to look at VIRGINIA.)

GLENN: No—

VIRGINIA: "Ladies on a Saturday walk"—

GLENN: No—

VIRGINIA: We're fifty-one percent of the population—

GLENN: Never mind—

VIRGINIA: Our day is near.

(VIRGINIA turns off the stereo. Music stops.)

GLENN: Don't have fun. Have a terrible time.

(GLENN watches as VIRGINIA puts on lipstick.)

VIRGINIA: Men are losing their grip, honey. We're
going to change things.

GLENN: Lipstick breaks down all kinds of barriers.

VIRGINIA: It doesn't hurt.
(She looks for her keys.)
Where are my keys?

GLENN: Probably where you left them.

(VIRGINIA just looks at GLENN.)

GLENN: What?

VIRGINIA: "Probably where you left them."

(VIRGINIA finally finds them in her shorts pocket. GLENN and VIRGINIA both smile.)

GLENN: See.

VIRGINIA: Jerk.
(She heads for the door.)

GLENN: Come here.

VIRGINIA: Why?

GLENN: I want to kiss you good-bye.

VIRGINIA: You already did.

GLENN: So I want to kiss you again.

VIRGINIA: You're not pulling me back to bed.

GLENN: Just come here.

(VIRGINIA quickly leans down. GLENN pulls her face close.)

GLENN: I love you, you know that?

VIRGINIA: Yes.

(GLENN kisses VIRGINIA.)

GLENN: You're beautiful.

VIRGINIA: I'm not coming back to bed.

GLENN: Can you please just pick up some chicken on the way home?

(VIRGINIA turns one of her signs around.)

(It reads, "EQUAL RIGHTS NOW!")

GLENN: It's a bucket of chicken.

VIRGINIA: Why am I in charge of dinner?

GLENN: I didn't say you were.

(VIRGINIA heads for the door.)

GLENN: Hey.

VIRGINIA: What?

GLENN: Be careful.

VIRGINIA: Honestly, Glenn—

GLENN: What?

VIRGINIA: "Be careful."

GLENN: What—

VIRGINIA: Must you say that every time I leave the house?

GLENN: What's wrong with it?

VIRGINIA: It makes me feel like a child.

GLENN: What *can* I say?

VIRGINIA: You respect me. You value me as an individual, as a person—that I'm more than just your wife and housekeeper and cook. More than just your lover.

GLENN: I have to say all that?

(VIRGINIA *just looks at* GLENN.)

(He laughs.)

VIRGINIA: It's not funny.
(She tries not to laugh.)

GLENN: It is a little bit.

VIRGINIA: You don't take me seriously.

GLENN: I do too. C'mon, honey. I'm just playing with you. Don't ruin a great afternoon with all this stuff. Relax—

VIRGINIA: I'm not ruining it. And this isn't "stuff", Glenn. I'm trying to change—

GLENN: I like who you are. You're perfect—

VIRGINIA: I'm trying to change things for other women—

GLENN: But you can't take a joke anymore.

VIRGINIA: Maybe some things just aren't as funny. Anymore.

GLENN: It's not my fault.
(Silence)
That's not my fault—

VIRGINIA: But you aren't helping.

GLENN: What do you want me to do?

VIRGINIA: Respect me—

GLENN: I don't know what else you want from me—

VIRGINIA: Do I have to ask for everything?

GLENN: You want me to go to Vietnam and look for him?

(VIRGINIA exits.)

GLENN: Virginia.

Scene 2

(Rally/march)

(VIRGINIA is joined by her sister, ALMA JENNINGS. They both hold signs, and wait for other women.)

(ALMA looks over VIRGINIA's outfit.)

ALMA: Did you forget your bra?

VIRGINIA: No.

(Silence)

ALMA: I hear that's popular in Europe.

VIRGINIA: It's popular a lot of places.

ALMA: It's tacky. Seeing so much…breast. In my opinion.

VIRGINIA: I didn't ask.

(Silence)

ALMA: You still going to Paris this summer?

VIRGINIA: That's the plan. Though I don't know how we're going to pay for it.

ALMA: Didn't Dad gave you some money for that?

VIRGINIA: We spent it.

ALMA: On what?

VIRGINIA: Glenn's tuition. And now we've put it off for three years, I think Glenn's only going because he feels guilty.

ALMA: It's your honeymoon, for Christ's sake.

VIRGINIA: I've read every book on France. Women have it much better there.

ALMA: I've never heard that.

VIRGINIA: Maybe we'll fall in love with Paris and never come back. Become painters or street musicians. Bohemians.

ALMA: What?

VIRGINIA: Street performers.

ALMA: Mimes?

VIRGINIA: No—

ALMA: Those people make me nervous. All that hand business.

VIRGINIA: No—

ALMA: Get out of the box already. You look ridiculous.

VIRGINIA: I'm not going to be a mime.

ALMA: Well, musicians? Please. What kind of instrument are you going to play?

VIRGINIA: Accordion. Trumpet. I don't know—

ALMA: You don't play those.

VIRGINIA: It's just a thought, Alma. A dream—

ALMA: Why would you want to live like that?

VIRGINIA: It sounds exciting. It would be different.

ALMA: Those people have B O.

VIRGINIA: They do not.

ALMA: It's a known fact. They stink.

VIRGINIA: Then I'll have B O.

ALMA: That's disgusting.

(VIRGINIA *moves her arm pit near* ALMA.)

ALMA: Gross. Don't!

(VIRGINIA *laughs.*)

ALMA: I just took a shower.

VIRGINIA: I just had sex.

ALMA: Get away from me.

(VIRGINIA *laughs harder.* ALMA *laughs with her.*)

ALMA: Go live in France.
(*She straightens herself.*)
I'm sure sex sweat is perfume in Paris.

VIRGINIA: I hope so.

ALMA: That's why we have soap, and bras, in America. It's chaos over there, Virginia. Nipples and chaos.

VIRGINIA: Good. I can't wait.
(She takes a good long look for ALMA's friends.)

(VIRGINIA looks at ALMA's watch.)

ALMA: They're coming. You're too impatient.

VIRGINIA: Did John give you this?

ALMA: He bought it on a business trip. It's not really me, but it's the thought. I guess.

VIRGINIA: I'm beginning to think Glenn is afraid to travel…I think he's afraid of a lot things.

ALMA: Like what?

VIRGINIA: Flying. Heights. Spices. Elevators. Bridges. Needles. Change.

ALMA: Everyone's afraid of those things.

VIRGINIA: Mice.

ALMA: Mice are nasty.

VIRGINIA: They're *this* big.

ALMA: So? They poop everywhere and carry diseases.

VIRGINIA: What disease have you caught from a mouse lately?

ALMA: You can never be too careful. Plague—

VIRGINIA: You and Glenn should get together.

ALMA: I'm starving. Is there going to be food at this thing?

VIRGINIA: It's a march not a picnic.

ALMA: But people have to eat.
(Silence)
I don't see anything wrong with a few snacks. Some chips or pretzels or something.

VIRGINIA: Where are they? Seriously. I'm going to lose my mind.

ALMA: Doris had to wait for her husband to come home from softball, and Judy had to wait for the baby-sitter, so—

VIRGINIA: That's always her excuse.

ALMA: Well, if you had kids you'd understand. Until I had Jason and Tracy—

VIRGINIA: I really look forward to that glorious day of transformation, when like a butterfly, I become anew because I have my "own children", and I get to feel that great wealth of knowledge and understanding and patience as it rushes over me like a long-lost river of "love I never knew was possible", and I am finally Finally equal and one with all women in motherhood, blank stares of disappointment, stifled discontent, late baby-sitters, and unending tardiness.

(Silence)

ALMA: Alright, Virginia.

(Silence)

I'm sorry.

(Silence)

Personally, I can't wait to be an aunt.

(Silence)

I think you'll make a terrific mother. You know how Tracy just adores you. When Glenn graduates and starts making some real money, you'll be able to have children, you can try again—

VIRGINIA: Maybe I don't want to be a mother.

ALMA: Don't say that.

VIRGINIA: Maybe they haven't all been miscarriages.

ALMA: What do you mean?

VIRGINIA: Maybe I'd rather just be an aunt.

ALMA: Virginia?

VIRGINIA: Never mind. Forgot it.

ALMA: I'm not going to forget it—

VIRGINIA: It doesn't matter. You wouldn't understand anyway. Fuck this, sorry, I'm not waiting anymore. I'm going ahead.

ALMA: They'll be here any minute.

VIRGINIA: I want to get a good spot.

ALMA: Good spot where?

VIRGINIA: Up with the leaders. The women who organized this thing. I want to meet them—

ALMA: Betty Friedan's here?

VIRGINIA: No, but—

ALMA: I thought she was in New York—

VIRGINIA: There are important women here too, Alma. It's our nation's capital. How do you think this thing happened?—

ALMA: It sounds dangerous.

VIRGINIA: How?

ALMA: You can never be too careful—

VIRGINIA: You careful people are going to kill me. I swear to God. I am being "careful"ed to death.

ALMA: Well, you never think ahead—

VIRGINIA: I'm thinking ahead right now. I want to go.

ALMA: What about us?

VIRGINIA: I'll meet up with you later.

(VIRGINIA *hands* ALMA *a pile of signs, and takes one for herself.*)

ALMA: No. Virginia…

VIRGINIA: I'll find you.

ALMA: Are you kidding? In all these people?

VIRGINIA: Meet me at Lincoln's feet.

ALMA: Lincoln Memorial? All the way over there?
I really wanted to do this together. As sisters. It's
important to me too, you know. This whole thing. I
think we're going to change things. If not for us, for
Tracy. Right? Higher pay and all that—

VIRGINIA: How do these women expect to have
equality if they can't even show up on time?

ALMA: Children are very demanding—

VIRGINIA: You think men wait?

ALMA: No, because they go ahead and do whatever the
hell they want, and let their wives take care of the kids.

VIRGINIA: Maybe, but—

ALMA: Just wait five more minutes.

VIRGINIA: All I ever do is wait—

ALMA: It's five minutes—

VIRGINIA: Wait on Glenn to finish school. Wait on
Glenn to go to Europe. Wait to save enough money to
do what I want. Wait for my brother to be found in the
jungle—

ALMA: Don't bring him into this now. I mean it. I'm not
in the mood—

VIRGINIA: Wait to start school. I had a math scholarship
I gave up—

ALMA: I know—

VIRGINIA: Wait my turn. Wait for my career to begin—
I'm a fucking waitress, for Christ's sake!
(*Silence*)

I have plans too. I have plans.

ALMA: It's not my fault.

VIRGINIA: EVERYTHING IS NOBODY'S FAULT?!
(Silence)
"It's not my fault" "It's not my fault". "It's not my
fault." That's all I hear anymore. It has got to be,
someone's fault, somewhere. Someone is responsible.
Someone has got to take responsibility for something.
Don't they? It is someone's fault. Isn't it? It is *someone's*
fault.

ALMA: You're getting hysterical. George will be
found—

VIRGINIA: I'm tired of wasting my life on other people's
schedules. I feel so…caught…lately.

ALMA: I'm asking you to wait five minutes. For me. I
don't think that will take so much time off your life.

VIRGINIA: I'll find you later.

ALMA: Virginia—

(VIRGINIA exits.)

Scene 3

(The March)

(Women and men are singing O S.)

(It's loud.)

(VIRGINIA is engulfed in people.)

*(She keeps her sign high. She is all smiles. Happy. Excited.
Free)*

VIRGINIA: Equality Now! Equality Now! Equality Now!
(This is the happiest, most alive she's felt in years.)
(The future is bright.)

(Suddenly something comes out of the blue.)

*(*VIRGINIA *turns, grabbing the back of her head, she's still smiling, not sure what happened.)*

(She goes down, falling, falling.)

(The music, the noise continues.)

Scene 4

*(*ALMA *waits at Lincoln's feet. Waiting. She checks her watch.)*

(Sound of an ambulance in the distance)

*(*ALMA *checks her watch again.)*

Scene 5

(Music)

*(*VIRGINIA *smiling. Her world has opened up. She is waving to her future. She is walking toward it.)*

(She is running toward it.)

(Blissful)

Scene 6

(The hospital)

*(*GLENN *is waiting.)*

*(*ALMA *rushes in.)*

ALMA: I got home and John said to go to the hospital…

*(*GLENN *just shakes his head.)*

ALMA: What happened?

GLENN: Someone threw a beer can into the crowd.

ALMA: A what?

GLENN: Beer can. Full of beer.

ALMA: Who?

GLENN: I don't know. Some redneck, I guess—

ALMA: Why?

GLENN: It hit Virginia... The doctor said she would
have been fine, but it knocked her off balance, and she
hit her head on the curb.

ALMA: Is she bleeding?

GLENN: There's, there's hemorrhaging. In the brain.
And swelling.

ALMA: How bad?

GLENN: They don't know yet.
(Silence)
Of all people, in a crowd of thousands, it had to hit
her?

ALMA: I told her it was dangerous.
(Silence)
Is she going to be okay?

GLENN: She's in a coma.
(Silence)

ALMA: Is she in pain?

GLENN: I don't know.

ALMA: Do Mother and Dad know? I didn't call them—

GLENN: They're on their way.

ALMA: God.
(Silence)
Why would someone do that?

GLENN: Drunk maybe. I don't know.
(Silence)

ALMA: Is she going to wake up?

GLENN: Of course.
(Silence)
She has to.

ALMA: Of course.
(She takes a seat beside him.)

GLENN: I was such an ass today. I don't know why. I just—

ALMA: She's going to be fine. I know it.

GLENN: I don't know why I act the way I do sometimes.
(Silence)
I couldn't just be nice? Easy?

ALMA: Virginia pushes people.

GLENN: I could have been easier. She's been so angry since George went missing. But she was excited about today. She was really excited. Hopeful.
(Silence)
I love her. She knows that, right?

ALMA: Of course.

GLENN: I respect her.
(Silence)
I do respect her. I just want her to know that.

ALMA: Of course.

Scene 7

(Music)

(Paris)

(GLENN enters playing an accordion.)

(VIRGINIA enters with a trumpet.)

(They play a sweet song.)
(Life is good.)

Scene 8

(1973)

(Hospital room)

(VIRGINIA in bed.)

(GLENN enters with flowers.)

GLENN: Hi Virginia.
(He moves close to the bed.)
(He holds the flowers under her nose.)
Nice, huh?
(He replaces the dead flowers beside her bed with the new ones.)
Lilies are expensive right now, but…
(Silence)
It's a special day.
(He smiles at her.)
(He pushes back her hair.)
Your hair is getting so long.
(He touches her face.)
Pretty soon we'll have to start calling you Rapunzel.
(Silence)
"Let down your long hair."
(Silence)
I'll climb up and rescue you.
(Silence)
Give me the chance.
(Silence)
Sleeping Beauty.
(Silence)
Snow White. ˙

(Silence)
Cinderella.
(He sits down.)
I know you hate that stuff. I'm sorry…
(Silence)
If you only knew how beautiful you looked.
(He takes a framed document from his briefcase.)
I didn't get a chance to show this to you last time. But I
thought you might want to see it.
(It's his diploma from Georgetown Law School.)
They forgot one of the n's in my name.
(He looks at the diploma.)
The only original idea my parents ever had, and yet,
seems I'm destined to be Glen with one n.
(He sets it by the bed.)
I wish you could have been at the ceremony. Your
parents came. Which was nice. And Alma brought the
kids. Jason is turning into a brat, honestly…and Tracy
barely talks and John just sits there and let's Alma do
everything…I'm afraid he may be having an affair…I
know you've never really trusted him…I don't think
she suspects anything. My parents didn't come. Said
they couldn't afford the trip. Typical, right? My dad
can afford a case a beer every night, but he can't afford
to drive to see his son graduate from law school.
(Silence)
Oh well.
(He thinks.)
I think I'm going to get a dog. A puppy.
(He smiles.)
Your mom thinks that will be good for me.
(Silence)
I like Collies.
(He thinks.)

Oh, hey, big news. They've legalized abortion. Roe versus Wade is the case that made it happen.
(*Silence*)
Thought you'd want to know that.
(*Silence*)
Thought you'd be happy to hear it.
(*Silence*)
We've pulled out of Vietnam. Officially. Or so they say. Did I already tell you that? I don't remember.
(*Silence*)
They have not found George. I'm sorry, honey. Apparently, there are a lot of men who are still missing in action.
(*Silence*)
They say it could be years.
(*Silence*)
I take the bar exam next week. Maybe I already told you that too? ...I'm sorry... Sometimes I can't remember what I've told you, and what I was thinking about telling you...I walk around the apartment all week thinking about things to tell you, and then I get here and forget them all or repeat myself.
(*Silence*)
I'm not sure I want to be a lawyer anymore. Which I probably shouldn't tell you, after all we paid to get me through school, but...we've always been honest with each other.
(*Silence*)
I'm not sure what I want to do with my life. I don't know what I care about anymore.
(*Silence*)
I guess I'll have to muddle through like everyone else, huh?
(*He smiles.*)
I'm sure it's just a feeling everyone gets at my age.

(Silence)
It'll pass.
(Silence)
I miss you.
(Silence)
Happy Anniversary.

Scene 9

(Music)

(Paris)

(VIRGINIA *is pregnant.*)

(GLENN *puts together a crib. He is dressed in French clothing.*)

(VIRGINIA *thumbs through a baby book.*)

VIRGINIA: Colette?

GLENN: No.

VIRGINIA: Claude?

GLENN: What's wrong with Mike? Mike is a good solid American name. Or Ginger. Ginger's good.

VIRGINIA: Ginger is a dog's name. Or a hooker.

GLENN: It is?

(VIRGINIA *suddenly sets the book aside.*)

VIRGINIA: Never mind.

GLENN: What?

VIRGINIA: I don't want it.

GLENN: What, no…Virginia.

(VIRGINIA *pulls the pillow from under her shirt.*)

GLENN: No, c'mon. Not again.

VIRGINIA: I changed my mind. I don't want a baby.

GLENN: Again?

VIRGINIA: I'm happy.

GLENN: But the baby will make you happy too.

VIRGINIA: You don't know that.

GLENN: It's common knowledge.

VIRGINIA: Since when is common knowledge the truth?

GLENN: You'll regret not having children.

VIRGINIA: Who says?

GLENN: Who is going to take care of you when you get old?

VIRGINIA: Is that a reason to have a kid? To make him or her, take care of me? To return the favor, the investment?

GLENN: No—

VIRGINIA: Sounds like buying insurance.
(She pushes the crib off the stage.)

GLENN: I want a family.

*(*VIRGINIA *returns with a suitcase.)*

GLENN: I want a baby with you.

VIRGINIA: There are plenty of women out there who want babies.

GLENN: I want a kid who has pieces of you and me. Parts of us.

VIRGINIA: I have things to do. Places I want to see. Plans.

GLENN: Like what?

VIRGINIA: What does it matter, what? Do I have to make a list? Do I have to justify myself?

GLENN: Yes. It would be nice.

VIRGINIA: I don't know why I keep getting caught here—

(She starts throwing things into the suitcase.)

VIRGINIA: Every time—

GLENN: Where are you going?

VIRGINIA: I keep getting caught in these same fucking boxes. I keep getting caught. I saw myself for the first time—I saw someone, something else one day...I saw her...I felt her: everything was possible...I was a million miles from here—

GLENN: Was I there?

(VIRGINIA just looks at GLENN.)

VIRGINIA: I wasn't talking about you.

GLENN: It's a simple question—

VIRGINIA: Can I please just go somewhere without you? Will you please let me, for one moment, be completely happy, outside of you?

GLENN: Well, if it was really fun I'd like to be there too. Can't you share?

VIRGINIA: No! I'm tired of sharing! I want it for myself! You come, and you start taking things. Piece by piece. You whittle me away. And then you start adding things I don't want.

GLENN: I'm just trying to help—

VIRGINIA: I don't want help.

GLENN: I love you. I just want you to know I love you.

VIRGINIA: This has nothing to do with love.

GLENN: I'll prove I love you. I respect you—

VIRGINIA: I don't want proof! I want freedom!

(Silence)

GLENN: I don't know why you're getting so worked up.

VIRGINIA: I want it to be different!

GLENN: What?

VIRGINIA: *This*. The picture. I can do anything I want now, can't I?

GLENN: Can you?—

VIRGINIA: And I'm doing *this*?

GLENN: What?

VIRGINIA: I got a glimpse of a place I'd never seen before. I could be anyone I wanted. I was flying so high, my chest felt like it was going to explode. I'd never felt that before. And yet, yet, here I am again. There is this cord that keeps tugging me back here. To this same fucking thing. You. Me. Rooms. Boxes. The crib. The baby names. *Your* dreams. *Your* future. I want out…I want to get out of here…George? George? Please? George?

GLENN: He's gone.

VIRGINIA: George?

GLENN: He's gone, Virginia.

VIRGINIA: George!

(GEORGE *enters in an Army uniform. He's handsome and clean cut.*)

GEORGE: Hi beautiful.

VIRGINIA: Oh George. You came.

GEORGE: Of course.

VIRGINIA: Look at you. Not a scratch on you. My sweet brother. Look at you. Perfect.

GEORGE: I feel pretty good.

VIRGINIA: I can't believe it.

GEORGE: Believe it. How's Alma?

VIRGINIA: I don't know.

GEORGE: I've missed you both.

VIRGINIA: Was the war awful?

GEORGE: Let's not talk about that.

VIRGINIA: Were you in pain?

GEORGE: Let's not talk about it.

VIRGINIA: I just want to know if you've been okay, George.

GEORGE: Don't worry.

VIRGINIA: I just need to need to know you're not hurting.

GEORGE: I've been looking all over for you.

GLENN: Hi George.

VIRGINIA: I was right here.

GEORGE: I've walked a million miles.

VIRGINIA: A million miles? That's funny. I think I was near there yesterday. I think it was yesterday…I don't remember—

GEORGE: You're kidding?

VIRGINIA: I only got to the edge.

GEORGE: We must have just missed each other.

VIRGINIA: Wow.

GEORGE: I know.

GLENN: Hi George.

VIRGINIA: What's it like out there? Past the edge. It felt so—

GEORGE: You wouldn't believe it if I told you.

VIRGINIA: Believe it good, or believe it bad?

GEORGE: You won't recognize yourself.

VIRGINIA: Will I still be pretty?

GEORGE: Gorgeous—

VIRGINIA: I want a thousand lovers.

GLENN: Where do you think you're going, the moon?

GEORGE: There's lots of men out there.

VIRGINIA: Let's go.

GEORGE: You sure you're ready?

VIRGINIA: Yes.

GLENN: George, please stop all this—

GEORGE: Oh, hey Glenn. Nice to see you.

GLENN: You too.

GEORGE: You gain weight?

(Silence)

GLENN: Maybe a little.

(Silence)

GLENN: I'm a lawyer now.

GEORGE: How's that working out for you?

GLENN: It's fine. But I want a family. I'm lonely.

VIRGINIA: He's not coming.

GEORGE: Sorry, man.

(They begin to exit.)

GLENN: When are you coming back?

VIRGINIA: Find someone else, Glenn.

GLENN: I don't want anyone else. I want you.

VIRGINIA: Please.

GLENN: I love you. I'll prove it to you—

VIRGINIA: I don't want your love. Stop keeping me here.

GLENN: I have to take care of you.

VIRGINIA: George, give me a hand here. I think you're going to have to help me.

(GEORGE *takes* VIRGINIA's *hand. Pulling her off stage*)

GLENN: Please come back, Virginia.

VIRGINIA: George, hurry. Get me out of here.

GLENN: Be careful.

VIRGINIA: (Jesus Christ with the careful.)

(GLENN *picks up the suitcase.*)

GLENN: Your suitcase?

(VIRGINIA *and* GEORGE *exit.*)

(GLENN *holds the suitcase.*)

(VIRGINIA *gets yanked back on stage.*)

VIRGINIA: I was so close.

(GLENN *looks at* VIRGINIA.)

VIRGINIA: Damn you.
(*She yells off stage.*)

GLENN: I love you.

VIRGINIA: George?

GEORGE: (O S) Yeah?

VIRGINIA: Come back, okay?

GEORGE: (O S) I'll see what I can do.

VIRGINIA: Come back and get me.

GEORGE: (O S) I can't promise anything.

VIRGINIA: And bring pictures. I want to see that place! I want to see that place out there, George!

GEORGE: *(O S)* Give my love to Alma.

VIRGINIA: I will. I'll try. But come back, okay? I need you.

GEORGE: *(O S)* Tell Glenn to start exercising. He's getting fat.

(GLENN rubs his stomach.)

VIRGINIA: I want to see that place!

Scene 10

(Hospital room)

(VIRGINIA in bed)

(1976)

(ALMA enters.)

ALMA: It's hot in here. Jesus Christ.
(She tries to open a window.)
I'm sorry I didn't come last week, but Tracy got sick (again) and then Jason was suspended from school so I had to stay home and keep an eye on him all day. Literally. All day. If I don't watch that kid day and night, he will break something, smoke something, or escape. I'm raising a criminal...I don't know where I went wrong—well, I didn't go wrong. It's John's fault. He has given his son no guidance whatsoever. If Jason ends up in Folsom Prison finding Jesus and making license plates, he will have his father to thank. I've done nothing but devote my life to that kid. And his little sister. Neither of them show me the slightest bit of appreciation. Thirteen and ten years old, and they talk to me like they're forty-five, drunk, and I'm their whore. Unbelievable, the language. If we had talked to mother and dad they way my kids talk to me, we

would not have a tooth left in our mouths, I'll tell you
that much. I don't know how I put up with it.
(She finally gives up on the window.)
Well, I know how I put up with it. I love them.
Obviously. They're the fruit of my loins… (Not the
best fruit, mind you, but…they're still my bananas) …
Those two martinis every night before dinner help.
Immensely.
(She smiles at VIRGINIA.*)*
Your hair is just about all grown back, huh? God, we
really thought we'd lost you that last time. But, you
held on…. You keep holding on. I tell Glenn, just let
her go…let you go.
(She takes a brush from her purse and begins to brush
VIRGINIA*'s hair, but brushes her own first.)*
Anyway…I'm letting my hair grow again. Every time I
get a new style, I hate it and John hates it, and we fight
because "he's a man that likes long hair so why can't
I just do one thing to make him happy", and I have
to remind him I do my share of things. To make him
happy. Most of which, he does not notice.
(She then brushes VIRGINIA*'s hair.)*
I wish I could just be like the Amish or something
and stick to one thing… To hell with fashion…I
would think that would be very freeing… Although,
they spend a lot of time churning butter and making
their own clothes and killing pigs and I don't have
the patience for all that… If I want bacon, I'll go to
the store for that, and I'm not going to churn my
own butter, for Christ's sake when someone else
can make it just as good. Though we've switched to
margarine. It's much better for you, and cheaper…
You wouldn't believe the price of things… How does
this country celebrate two hundred years? What's
our big bicentennial present? Inflation… Thank you,
Uncle Sam… We finally get out of Vietnam, and now

we all have to pay for it…as if we hadn't paid enough
already…I think it's what's given mother cancer…
And I think Dad is going to drink himself to death one
day… Sometimes I think they look at me and wonder
what happened, where'd all their kids go? …One
minute they had three, and the next I'm standing at
their front door holding a bundt cake, all by myself…I
catch Mother looking behind me, looking for you and
George…and then when it's my kids who walk up,
she can't hide her disappointment. I get it. I often look
at my kids and think, "where'd these creeps come
from?"…John is a terrible father… Oh, gosh, I almost
forgot…juicy gossip…I had a cup of coffee with my
friend Judy before I came over here—you remember
Judy…

(She stops brushing.)

Of course you do. If you had just waited on her,
maybe, maybe, all this would have been different.
Maybe. Not that I'm blaming Judy. Or you… But…
it was a few minutes, Virginia. Really. A few minutes.
You really are the most impatient person I've ever
met…

(She resumes brushing.)

Anyway, Judy said she needed to *talk*. Which is code
for my husband is leaving me. Or I'm pregnant. Or so
and so tried to kill herself. Or, do you have any pink
pills to spare. So, I go over there…Turns out, she's
having an affair with someone, she wouldn't tell me
who, and he won't leave his wife, and she can't leave
her husband because she never went to college, and
has no skills, and is afraid of landing in the gutter. She
and her husband were high-school sweethearts, but
she says she really loves this other guy, so she's all
wrung out and I ended up giving her one of the pills
the dentist gave me when I had that root canal last
year as I do find they help most things. (I've had the

prescription refilled four times.) I really didn't know
what to tell her. I mean, I do have a college degree
but what good has it done me? Have I used it? Who
really gives a rats ass about English Literature? What's
someone going to hire me to do, recite Beowolf for
three dollars an hour? Save lives with Shakespeare
sonnets? Solve world hunger with my paper on Mary
Shelly? Yeah, there's about a snowballs chance in hell
of that happening. I don't have any more skills than
Judy does now...It all makes you think... Does anyone
know what the hell they're doing? ...Maybe those
Amish have it all figured out and we just don't know
it...you never hear about them getting stuck in affairs,
looking for careers, or sticking their head in an oven to
end it all.
(Silence)
Of course they cook with wood.

Scene 11

(Music)

(Paris)

*(VIRGINIA is a professor. She gives a lecture in French,
points to a large math problem on a chalk board, and smiles.
Points to a student in the distance)*

VIRGINIA: Oui?

Scene 12

(1981)

(New nursing home room.)

(VIRGINIA's body is turned toward the wall.)

*(GLENN hangs some pictures on the wall. He is wearing a
nice suit.)*

GLENN: The nurses told me you moved your eyelids yesterday.

(Silence)

I wonder what you were thinking about.

(Silence)

Maybe it was Ronald Reagan's inauguration. What kind of country elects an B movie actor to be President? Seriously? …The cream does not rise to the top in America, Virginia..It curdles somewhere near the bottom of California, and we get guys like Reagan.

(He stands back to look at his picture hanging skills.)

I know this new room feels different than the last, but it's closer to my house, and the care is very good here.

(He points to one of the pictures.)

That's my house. Our house. Not shabby, huh? You can't see if from this view, but it's got a huge back yard. All fenced. The dogs loves it. And it's got a screen porch off the back that is wonderful in the summer. I sit out there and read the paper. Your sister tells everyone it's a mansion. She exaggerates. As you know.

(He points to another picture.)

Those are my dogs. Mutt and Jeff.

(He points to another picture.)

This is a family gathering we had when your nephew Jason got out of reform school. He stole all the liquor out of my liquor cabinet, so I'm not sure much reforming went on there.

(He takes a closer look.)

I don't know why Tracy isn't in the picture…huh…she must have been inside or something. Your dad looks miserable. It was the first family gathering since your mother died. We drank a lot that day. (Before Jason stole what was left of it.)

(He points to a picture of Paris.)

I didn't take this one. This is France. One of the
partners from the law firm went to Paris last year and
took this picture. I thought you'd like it, so I asked him
for a copy. He said he and his wife had a terrific time.
(He points to one last picture. Their wedding picture)
And here's an oldie but a goody. Look at us. Jesus.
Kids. Look at my hair. Looks like I'm growing a wig...
Look how beautiful you look. God. How'd I get so
lucky, I thought. She picked me? With that hair? ...I
cried my eyes out that day, remember?
(He straightens the picture.)
I promised you a house with a big yard. A place for
kids and dogs, where everyone feels welcome. A home.
I promised it all. And I got it.

Scene 13

(Music)

(Paris)

(VIRGINIA sits across from GEORGE at a sidewalk cafe.)

VIRGINIA: Thanks for meeting me here. I can't see you
at home, as you know. What happened last time.

GEORGE: Yeah.

VIRGINIA: I miss you, George.

GEORGE: You look great.

VIRGINIA: You too. Muscular.

GEORGE: I've been working out.

(Silence)

VIRGINIA: I need you to do me a favor.

GEORGE: What are brothers for?

VIRGINIA: France is nice, and I've enjoyed the wine and the men (I've been having affairs.) I've got a great career.

GEORGE: Who you having affairs with?

VIRGINIA: My students. I'm teaching now.

GEORGE: Wow.

VIRGINIA: But, I'm wondering if I'm done here.

GEORGE: Done.

VIRGINIA: Maybe it's time to move on.

GEORGE: Good idea. Go home.

VIRGINIA: Or…You could take me with you.

(Silence)

GEORGE: I don't know, Virginia…

VIRGINIA: You said it was so great out there. "I wouldn't recognize myself…."

GEORGE: I may have exaggerated. A bit. For affect.

VIRGINIA: What do you mean?

GEORGE: It's boring.

VIRGINIA: Boring?

GEORGE: After you get that initial rush, and feel all the lightness and freedom from all your pain and suffering and earthly worries, etc… It's…remarkably…dull.

VIRGINIA: You're just saying that to keep me here—

GEORGE: I started lifting weights because I don't know what else to do with all my endless, endless time, but get bigger. Stronger. And the irony is, there's no one to touch this new me. We all just float right through each other. Like cartoons. Men, women, we just float right through each other, not a real care in the world…ships passing in the endless night. Vacant.

VIRGINIA: So everyone's equal?

GEORGE: But there's no friction. No strife. Nothing. It's frustrating—

VIRGINIA: Sounds peaceful.

GEORGE: No. It's hell. There are all these beautiful men out there. Paradise, Virginia... Paradise... But, it's all air. Open space... Mist... We're beyond the beyond...We're shells of what we used to be...And the angels who buzz around everywhere, like naked, giggly gnats? Excruciating... Believe me. You want some tension. Something hard to push up against... Something very hard.
(He sighs)
I miss my body.

(Silence)

GEORGE: You're better off here. Trust me.

VIRGINIA: I don't know what to do next.

GEORGE: You have your body. Enjoy it.

VIRGINIA: I'm afraid I'm wasting my life.

GEORGE: Please. That's all I hear out there, "Did I waste my life", "Did my life mean anything?" "Should I have done more?", "Did I do anything Important?" ... "Did I die in vain?", "Did I die in vain?", "Did I die in vain?"
(Silence)
Did I?

VIRGINIA: What?

GEORGE: Die in vain?

(Silence)

(GEORGE looks at his arm, flexes his muscle, out of habit.)

VIRGINIA: Am I *living* in vain?
(Silence)

George?

GEORGE: Huh?

VIRGINIA: Am I living in vain?

GEORGE: You still have your body. Anything's possible.

(VIRGINIA *looks at herself.*)

GEORGE: You're not done. Use it.

VIRGINIA: How? What am I supposed to do next? I thought a career would make me happy, but it's not enough—

GEORGE: Go home.

VIRGINIA: I don't want to go back. Not yet. Take me with you.

GEORGE: No.

VIRGINIA: I think it sounds so lovely. Free—

GEORGE: No.

VIRGINIA: But—

GEORGE: What about Alma?

VIRGINIA: What about her?

GEORGE: And Glenn?

VIRGINIA: What about me? What I want? Please, George. Take me—

GEORGE: No.
(*He checks his muscle on more time.*)
Now if you'll excuse me…
(*He gets up. Sighs*)
I gotta go pump some iron.
(*He exits.*)

Scene 14

(Nursing home room)

(1985)

(ALMA holds a cake with a 40 candle on it. GLENN holds balloon.)

(They blow out the candle together.)

ALMA: Welcome to middle age.

GLENN: Stop.

ALMA: You are now officially over the hill, Virginia.

GLENN: Don't say that.

ALMA: It's true.

(GLENN ties the balloons to the bed.)

GLENN: Says who?

ALMA: Everyone.

GLENN: Who's everyone?

ALMA: Everyone.

GLENN: Who are they? I want names.

ALMA: *Time* magazine.

GLENN: Please.

ALMA: Did you bring a knife?

GLENN: No. Did you?

ALMA: No. I wasn't in charge of the cake.

GLENN: You want a piece?

ALMA: I'm watching my weight.

GLENN: Me too.

(ALMA and GLENN admire the cake.)

(They continue to stare at the cake.)

ALMA: Well, I'll put it over here. The nurses will eat it. Is it vanilla or chocolate?

GLENN: Vanilla.

ALMA: Why didn't you get chocolate?

GLENN: I don't know—

ALMA: Virginia always had chocolate cake.

(GLENN *just looks at* ALMA.)

GLENN: They were out.

ALMA: Well.

GLENN: You can buy the cake next time.

ALMA: You're the one with all the money.
(Silence)
Her skin looks dry. Are they moisturizing enough?

GLENN: I think so—

ALMA: A woman hits forty, and you really gotta start lathering on the lotion. I mean it. The battle against wrinkles is on. It's like fighting the Vietnamese. They're crafty, they come out of no where, and they'll win.

GLENN: Uh huh.

ALMA: I'm serious. And they're still massaging her legs and arms, right? They gotta keep her body moving. You gotta keep everything moving at this age.

GLENN: I pay for that.

ALMA: Well you should just make sure they are actually doing it here. People will rip you off, Glenn. You're too trusting. You turn around, and people will rob you blind if you aren't careful.

GLENN: Your son took my watch.

ALMA: What?

GLENN: When you all came over to drop off that casserole last week, and Jason asked to use the rest room...

ALMA: Yeah.

GLENN: He took my gold watch that I left sitting by the sink.

ALMA: Why'd you leave it there?

GLENN: It's my fault?

ALMA: Why would you leave a nice gold watch in the bathroom?

GLENN: Because it's my house.

ALMA: You know how Jason is.

GLENN: A crook?

ALMA: Yes.

GLENN: Well, tell him I want it back. It was a gift.

ALMA: From who?

GLENN: Just tell him I want it back.

(Silence)

(GLENN looks at VIRGINIA.)

ALMA: Glenn?

GLENN: I'm not going to discuss this here.

(ALMA pulls GLENN away from VIRGINIA to the far side of the room.)

ALMA: Are you having sex?
(Silence)
You better be wearing a condom. *Time* magazine did a big story on this AIDS epidemic going around—

GLENN: Please. That's your sister over there.

ALMA: In a coma. Who you won't let die.

GLENN: Don't start.

ALMA: Surely there have been others.
(*Silence*)
You can't be a complete saint. And I'm mean it about
the condoms and the AIDS thing. You can't be too
careful—

GLENN: No one serious.

ALMA: Is this woman serious?

(*Silence*)

GLENN: She lives in New York.

ALMA: Does she have a family?

GLENN: She has a career. In finance. She's very
successful.

ALMA: That's too bad.

GLENN: Why?

ALMA: It would be nice if you could be a father.

GLENN: I have dogs.

ALMA: It's not the same.
(*Silence*)
Personally, I don't know how you do it.

GLENN: What?

ALMA: This.

GLENN: She's my wife.

ALMA: Of course, but—

GLENN: I made a promise—

ALMA: You were nineteen—

GLENN: I'm not going to—

ALMA: Who knew what sickness and health really
meant at that age?

GLENN: I'm not going to be the man who abandons his wife.

ALMA: John and I made promises to each other. Did we keep them? To honor and to hold? He's "honored and held" everything that moves in his office... He forgets that I do the laundry.

GLENN: Yet you stay with him.

ALMA: What am I going to do, leave him, leave my delinquent kids, get a job, start all over? At my age?

GLENN: You're forty-five.

ALMA: Exactly.
(She walks over to the cake and begins eating it with her fingers.)

GLENN: If you need financial help, Alma, I'll give it to you. If you wanted to leave. I'll help you.

ALMA: Become a divorcee? Live alone? No thank you.

GLENN: So what—

ALMA: You tell me to leave, but you insist on playing martyr.

GLENN: This is different.

(Silence)

ALMA: I have a good life.
(Silence)
Happiness isn't everything.
(She keeps eating the cake.)

Scene 15

(Music)

(Paris)

(GLENN plays a sad song on the accordion.)

(VIRGINIA *stands beside her suitcase.*)

VIRGINIA: Happiness is everything.

(GLENN *keeps playing.*)

VIRGINIA: Right, Glenn?

(GLENN *keeps playing.*)

VIRGINIA: Glenn.

GLENN: Pardon?
(*He stops playing the accordion.*)
I'm sorry. What did you say?

VIRGINIA: I want to be happy. Don't you?

GLENN: I am happy.

VIRGINIA: Really?

GLENN: I think. I think so. Yes.

(VIRGINIA *picks up her suitcase, and walks over and kisses* GLENN.)

VIRGINIA: There's a whole world out there, Glenn. A whole world.

(VIRGINIA *exits.* GLENN *watches her go.*)

(*He continues to play the accordion, an even sadder song than before.*)

Scene 16

(*Hospital*)

(*1996*)

(*A nurse,* SUSAN JONES *brings in a birthday cake, a newspaper under her arm.*)

(*She shows the cake to* VIRGINIA.)

SUSAN: Your husband sent this over. He wanted me to tell you he's sorry he couldn't make it. He had to go

to a conference in New York. Again. And your sister
called to say that her son Jason's trial was today, so…
(She puts it beside the bed.)
Looks like you're spending the big fifty-one with me,
Mrs Moore.
(She tastes the cake.)
I spent my thirtieth birthday with my husband last
year, and ended up taking him to the hospital for
alcohol poisoning. So, celebrating with family isn't all
it's cracked up to be. It was four days before he could
get out of bed and give me my present. And what did
he give me when he did? A toaster oven.
(She opens the paper.)
I told him if he thinks I'm going to toast anything for
him, he can kiss my ass. Just once I'd like him to plan
something special or give me something romantic,
something I actually want. He uses my birthday as an
excuse to get the things we need around the house…I
got an electric drill for two years ago. What do I want
with a drill?
(Silence)
Of course I don't mind a good drilling. If the mood is
right.
(She winks at VIRGINIA.)
He is very good at that. He is very giving there, I guess.
Makes up for a lot.
(She smiles.)
I bet you miss that. I bet you miss a lot of things.
Maybe one of these days you'll wake up and come out
here and grab them, huh? I keep praying for you. I
know you're in there. I know it. Waiting.
(She skims the newspaper.)
Let's see what the news is today… They keep talking
about this computer internet thing…electronic mail…
say it's going to catch on real big…I don't know…

Sounds like a big waste of time to me. Who wants to sit behind a computer all day and have to deal with that nonsense? Not me.
(She sighs.)
Let's skip ahead to the horoscope…
(She finds the right page. Reads)
"The heavens are shifting, Gemini. Get ready…This is a new start.."

Scene 17

(Music)

(Europe)

(VIRGINIA is traveling on a long road. She carries books, a hat, and her suitcase. She is happy.)

(She stops when she finds several pairs of small children's shoes. With a note attached. She picks up the note.)

VIRGINIA: *(Reading)* "From the children you didn't have. We found other mothers. Thank you."
(She picks up one of the shoes and looks at it closer. It's a girl's mary-jane.)
(She puts it in her suitcase.)
(She finds one more shoe. A little sneaker. With another note.)
(Reading)
"Alma's child she didn't have. Tell her thank you."
(She leaves the shoe, and continues on.)

Scene 18

(2001)

(Nursing home room.)

(VIRGINIA lies in bed. The T V is on.)

(GLENN, ALMA, *and* SUSAN *sit glued with eyes on the television. Reports of the 9/11 attacks*)

ALMA: We saw that man running two minutes ago. They're just showing the same video, over and over again.

SUSAN: I can't stop watching.

(Silence)

ALMA: I just wish they'd get some new pictures. I mean, really. Do we have to see the planes go into the buildings over and over again?

(They keep watching.)

(Long silence)

ALMA: It's a good thing we have George Bush.

(GLENN *and* SUSAN *look at* ALMA.)

(GLENN *and* SUSAN *look at each other. He shakes his head.*)

ALMA: Oh, you think if Gore had won this wouldn't have happened?

GLENN: Let's not get into it.

ALMA: Gore—

GLENN: I mean it, Alma. I'm not in the mood.
(He dials his cell phone.)

ALMA: Jason called me from Germany to say the Army's been put on high alert.

GLENN: After what your family went through with your brother, I can't believe you let your only son enlist—

ALMA: *Let? Let?* The judge ordered it. It was his last chance. It was prison or the Army. And I tell you what, it's been the best thing to ever happen to that kid. Turned him around.

GLENN: He never did return that watch.

ALMA: You survived, didn't you?

(GLENN *gets nothing on his phone.*)

ALMA: Who are you trying to call?

(*They all turn their attention to the T V again.*)

ALMA: They're barely talking about the plane that went into the Pentagon. About what happened here. It's not fair. It's all about New York. Picture after picture of New York.

(*More watching*)

ALMA: See? More New York. New York, New York, New York—

GLENN: Please shut up.

(*Silence*)

ALMA: Pardon?

GLENN: You've been jabbering on all morning. I can't take it anymore.
(*He dials his cell phone again.*)

ALMA: Well excuse me. Mr Sensitive—

GLENN: What does it matter what pictures they show on T V? It's all awful, isn't it?

ALMA: Of course—

GLENN: Then stop commenting on every fucking thing. The country has just had the floor fall out from under it, and you're worried about what's fair? What pictures we get to see more of?

ALMA: I don't know—

GLENN: People have died. The country has changed. Don't you get it? ...Everything's different now.
(*He gets no answer on his phone.*)

ALMA: It's not my fault.

(GLENN *slams his phone shut.*)

GLENN: I didn't say it was.

(*They keep watching.*)

(GLENN *puts his head in his hands.*)

Scene 19

(*Music*)

(*The desert*)

(VIRGINIA *wears a scarf covering her face. She puts down her suitcase, and removers her scarf to see what's left from a road side bomb. A man's boot. A woman's bloody scarf. A small American flag*)

(*At the same time on stage:*)

(*A young woman,* TRACY JENNINGS *enters the nursing home room and stands at the door. She stands for a moment, looking at* VIRGINIA's *still body in bed.*)

TRACY: Aunt Virginia. My mother needs you.
(*Unable to go inside, she walks away.*)

Scene 20

(*2005*)

(*Nursing home room*)

(VIRGINIA *in bed.*)

(GLENN *takes down the pictures on the wall.*)

GLENN: The good thing is, Susan will still be your nurse. She'll be at the new facility.

(GLENN *takes down the picture of his dogs. It's dusty.*)

GLENN: The surgery won't take long. The doctors think it's the best thing to do.

(He takes down their wedding picture. And the picture of his house.)

The house should sell fast. In this market. I should get some money out it.

(He looks at the pictures again.)

I don't know what I'm going to do with all my stuff.

I guess I'll have to have a garage sale or something.

Maybe I can get Alma to help me. It might be good for her.

(He takes down the family photo.)

She hasn't left the house since Jason was killed.

(He looks at the photo.)

The Army have gave him a big funeral at Arlington.

(Silence)

He was still wearing my gold watch.

Scene 21

(Music)

(The ocean)

(VIRGINIA is dressed in the clothes of her travels. She carries her suitcase, more books and treasures.)

VIRGINIA: George? George?

GEORGE: *(O S)* What?

VIRGINIA: Alma needs help.

GEORGE: *(O S)* I'm not an angel, Virginia.

VIRGINIA: Alma needs help.

GEORGE: *(O S)* You're the one with the body. Go help her.

VIRGINIA: Have you seen Jason?

GEORGE: *(O S)* It's a vast expanse out here, not a Carnival Cruise.

VIRGINIA: Well, I'm sure Alma would like it if you kept an eye out for him.

GEORGE: *(O S)* I'll see what I can do.

VIRGINIA: George?

(Silence)

George?!

GEORGE: *(O S)* I'm kinda right in the middle of something—

VIRGINIA: You wouldn't believe the things I've seen.

GEORGE: *(O S)* Uh huh.

VIRGINIA: I've traveled the world. I've experienced freedom. Real freedom. I know who I am, George. There is nothing holding me back. The boxes are gone. You can't imagine what that's like...well, it's wonderful.

GEORGE: *(O S)* Uh huh.

(Silence)

VIRGINIA: But...but, sometimes, lately, I do feel a lonely. I wonder what Glenn might have thought of all the places I've been; what he would see that would be different and new...I wonder if I should have children...Someone to share life with...What do you think?

(Silence)

George?

(Silence)

I never thought I'd want children, but I do. I'm changing. I didn't think there was enough of me to give in the past. I had too much to do and see. I had plans, right? But there's enough now... There's plenty...I wonder how would this world look through a child's eyes? What could a child teach me? Who would I be as a mother?

(Silence)

Do you think I'd be a good mother?

(Silence)

George?

(GEORGE enters, sweaty. He's carrying small bar bells.)

VIRGINIA: There you are. I'm always so happy to see you. Wow, look at those muscles.

GEORGE: It's too late, Virginia.

VIRGINIA: Too late for what?

GEORGE: Children.

(Silence)

VIRGINIA: What do you mean?

GEORGE: You're too old.

VIRGINIA: Too old? …No, no…I have a body. Look.
(Silence)
You said, I still have body. "Use it."

GEORGE: I know, but not—

VIRGINIA: Look at me. I'm ready. I understand who I am—

GEORGE: Not for that.

(Silence)

VIRGINIA: But—

GEORGE: That's not the world, Virginia. Where you are. Where you've been—

VIRGINIA: What is it?

GEORGE: That's not…this isn't life.

VIRGINIA: What is it?

GEORGE: You need to let me go. And go home.

VIRGINIA: Why?

GEORGE: Go home. Go while you still have a chance.

VIRGINIA: A chance for what?
(Silence)
A chance for what?

GEORGE: To live.

VIRGINIA: But—

GEORGE: A chance to see Alma. Glenn. Tracy. Life.

VIRGINIA: It aches when I think of them. It aches already.

GEORGE: I wish I could ache. I miss it...Go while you still have a chance.

VIRGINIA: I've felt so free.

GEORGE: I'd do anything to feel that pain.

VIRGINIA: Maybe, maybe I should just go with you. Maybe—

GEORGE: No.

VIRGINIA: What if it's too much?

GEORGE: Oh, to feel that again...the ache of love...*that* is life.
(He begins to exit.)
I envy you.
(He exits.)

VIRGINIA: George? What if it's too much?

GEORGE: *(O S)* Then you're alive again, Virginia! What I'd give to be you!

VIRGINIA: George?

Scene 22

(2011)

(Different nursing home)

*(*VIRGINIA *in a bed in small corner of the stage.)*

*(*SUSAN *moves around the small space to change the bedsheets under* VIRGINIA.*)*

SUSAN: Now they're all up in the President's ass because they think he's not doing enough. Doing enough? Jesus Christ. The man inherited a shit box. It took the last guy eight years to mess things up, and they want the new guy to come fix it all in three. He's a man not a magician. No one's ever satisfied. It's a country full of people who always want the other guy to do all the work, while they sit home and watch television and eat nachos. The whole country is sitting in front of their flat screen T Vs, stuffing their faces, waiting for everyone else to fix all their problems. War. Healthcare. Unemployment. I have worked my whole goddamn life, and you know who is responsible for me? You know who's going to fix my problems? Me and my two hands. That's what I was given in this country. That's it... Hell, at least I have my hands... my mother sat on hers in the back of the bus, and her mother's hands got buried in a field of cotton, and her mother's, bound in chains... They didn't even have the right to their own hands...
(She holds up hands.)
This is progress.
(She checks her manicure, fluffs a pillow, gets back to work.)
I know government can't do it all. No president can do it alone. Everyone got all excited about all the Change that was coming to this country, all the Hope, and then when they realized *they* might have to Change, *they* might have to keep that Hope alive and do something,

sacrifice something, get off the couch, for longer than
a month or two, nope, sorry, they were done. They
gave all they were willing to give to the idea, and now
the President is dragging around all that Hope and
Change like a bag of rocks, no one wants to help him
lift. They want to criticize him, but they don't want
to do the work to help him lift all those hopes and
dreams. I swear to God, Mrs Moore, if I could just
have one moment in the sun, one moment where my
voice could be heard across the land, on the news, on
the radio, on the internet, I would give this country
a piece of my mind and say, WAKE THE FUCK UP!
WAKE UP! What are you people waiting for? Daddy
to come take care of you? Mommy to wipe your chin?
Well, Daddy's not coming. Mommy's out standing in
line for food stamps. Wake up and take responsibility
for yourself. This is your country. Act like you love
it. Do something. ACT! You don't like corporations
running everything, don't buy that corporation's shit.
You don't have a job, you don't like that we're fighting
these wars, get in the streets and demand to be heard.
And when you get in the streets, know what to ask for!
Be specific! Don't just "occupy" —rise up! Get off your
fat asses and give your President a country to lead, and
then when you've actually Participated in something,
when you've got your hands dirty, made something
happen for someone else, for the better good, not just
bitched about it, then you have the right to sit back
down on that couch and wait for your ass to grow and
your nachos to cool. You know what I mean?

VIRGINIA: Please call me Virginia.

SUSAN: Mrs Moore?

VIRGINIA: Virginia.

(VIRGINIA *is awake.*)

END OF ACT ONE

ACT TWO

Scene 1

(Months later)

(Washington, DC)

(GLENN's small, humble apartment)

(A couch, a big screen T V, a desk with a computer, a small kitchen table.)

(GLENN opens the door and pushes VIRGINIA into the room in a wheel chair.)

GLENN: Here we are.

(VIRGINIA takes in the room.)

GLENN: Like I said, I downsized. It's no castle, but I find I have most everything I need.

(GLENN smiles and stops the wheelchair, and walks in front of VIRGINIA. Looks at the room with her)

VIRGINIA: It's, it's very nice.

(GLENN suddenly sees the room through VIRGINIA's eyes.)

GLENN: I sometimes wonder if I maybe downsized a size too small. But, less is more, I guess... Less is more.
(Silence)
Well then. Welcome home.
(Silence)
Can I make you a cup of tea? Or coffee?

VIRGINIA: Oh. Coffee. Please. Thank you.

GLENN: Coffee it is. Coming right up.

(GLENN *exits and* VIRGINIA *looks around again at the room.*)

(*This is her new home: this small, foreign room, her new life.*)

(GLENN *enters with a plate of cookies.*)

GLENN: You like chocolate chip?

VIRGINIA: Pardon?

GLENN: They're from a box. I have to wait for the coffee to brew.

VIRGINIA: Would it be possible to open a window?

GLENN: I have the heat on.

VIRGINIA: Oh.
(*Silence*)
I'm sorry, but I just need a little fresh air. If you don't mind.

(GLENN *walks over to a window.*)

GLENN: I never open these windows. I have central air. Let me see here.
(*He tries to open a window. It doesn't budge.*)
I think it's painted shut.
(*He keeps trying. Grunting*)

VIRGINIA: I don't want you to hurt yourself.

(GLENN *tries banging it with his shoe.*)

VIRGINIA: That's ok. Really.

(GLENN *finally gives up, exhausted.*)

VIRGINIA: It doesn't matter. I'll, I'll be fine.

GLENN: You sure?
(*He looks at the window again. Defeated*)

VIRGINIA: Positive.

GLENN: I'll turn the heat down.
(He puts his shoe back on.)

VIRGINIA: That will probably do it. Thank you.

(GLENN walks over and adjusts the thermostat, then sits across from VIRGINIA on the couch. Trying to get his breath and composure)

GLENN: I tend to run cold.
(He takes out his handkerchief and wipes the sweat from his forehead.)

(Silence)

VIRGINIA: I like how you've decorated the place.

(GLENN is still attending to his forehead, and refolding his handkerchief.)

VIRGINIA: Is that your television?

GLENN: Pardon?

VIRGINIA: That's your television?

GLENN: Yeah. It's high definition.

VIRGINIA: High Definition. I see.
(Silence)
It's very large.

GLENN: That's how they make them now. You wouldn't believe the color on that thing. You want me to turn it on? Show you the picture?

VIRGINIA: No, no.

GLENN: Are you sure?

VIRGINIA: Not right now. Thank you.
(Silence)
You relax.

GLENN: It's great for sports. You feel like you're right there.

VIRGINIA: I imagine.

(Silence)

(GLENN eats a cookie.)

VIRGINIA: And that's your computer?

GLENN: Uh huh.

VIRGINIA: I still can't get over it. What a world.

GLENN: You want me to show you how to use it? It's real easy—

VIRGINIA: Not yet. Thank you.
(Silence)
Maybe at another time.

GLENN: I bet this all seems pretty crazy to you.

VIRGINIA: What?

GLENN: Technology.

VIRGINIA: A bit.

GLENN: You've been in a time warp.

VIRGINIA: I guess you could call it that.
(She smiles.)

(Silence)

GLENN: Is it hard to get used to seeing me like this?

VIRGINIA: Like what?

GLENN: Old.

VIRGINIA: No, not really—

GLENN: I lost my hair.
(He tries to pad down the hair he has left.)

VIRGINIA: I see that.

GLENN: What can you do?

VIRGINIA: Not much, really.

(Silence)

It's distinguished.

GLENN: I'm not the toupee type.
(He stops padding down his hair.)
You still look beautiful.

VIRGINIA: Do I?

GLENN: Oh, let me go get that coffee. I almost forgot.

(VIRGINIA touches her face. Her hair)

(GLENN exits to the kitchen. Returns with two cups)

GLENN: It's decaf. No one drinks regular at this hour.

VIRGINIA: They don't?

GLENN: Not at our age.

VIRGINIA: Why not?

GLENN: No one wants to be up half the night.

(GLENN and VIRGINIA drink.)

GLENN: Sleep is important.

VIRGINIA: Might you have cream? For the coffee.

GLENN: I thought you took it black.

VIRGINIA: No.

GLENN: You used to.

VIRGINIA: Not anymore.

GLENN: Oh. Okay.
(Silence)
I don't have any cream.

VIRGINIA: That's fine.

GLENN: I can get some tomorrow.

VIRGINIA: This is fine.

GLENN: I'm sorry.

VIRGINIA: It's not a problem.

(Silence)

GLENN: I'll put that on my list. I'll go to the grocery store tomorrow.

VIRGINIA: It's not a problem. Really.

(Silence)

GLENN: I guess I just assumed you'd like the same things.

VIRGINIA: No.

(GLENN tries to smile. VIRGINIA matches his attempt.)

(Silence)

VIRGINIA: Is Alma coming soon? I think it's strange I haven't seen her yet—

GLENN: She's been out of town.

VIRGINIA: Where?

GLENN: She didn't tell me, but I'm sure she's anxious to see you.

VIRGINIA: How is she?

GLENN: Jason was killed in Iraq.

VIRGINIA: Yes. You told me.

GLENN: I never really trusted you could hear me.

VIRGINIA: I could.

GLENN: Anti-depressants have done Alma a world of good.

VIRGINIA: Really?

GLENN: I take them too. You'd be amazed how far medicine has come. Kept you alive, didn't it?
(He smiles.)

VIRGINIA: This is true.
(Silence)
Are John and Alma doing alright?

GLENN: Sure.

VIRGINIA: And Tracy?

GLENN: What about her?

VIRGINIA: No one ever talks about her. I haven't seen her—

GLENN: She's a doctor now, I think.

VIRGINIA: Really? What kind of doctor?

GLENN: She's been estranged from them for years.

VIRGINIA: Why?

GLENN: There's so much to catch up on, I don't know where to start.

VIRGINIA: Will I get to see Tracy? I'd like to see her—

(GLENN grabs VIRGINIA's hand. She looks at his hand on hers.)

GLENN: Where do we start?

VIRGINIA: I don't know.
(Silence)
May I use your rest room?

GLENN: Now?

VIRGINIA: Please.

GLENN: Oh. Okay. Sure. Sure.
(He gets up.)

VIRGINIA: Thank you.

GLENN: It's right over here.

(GLENN pushes VIRGINIA across the room, opens a door.)

GLENN: You need some help.

VIRGINIA: No.

GLENN: Are you sure?

VIRGINIA: I think I can do it. Thank you.

GLENN: Are you sure? You're still—

VIRGINIA: I'll be fine.

GLENN: You're sure now?

VIRGINIA: Thank you.
(She closes the door.)

(GLENN stays by the door.)

Scene 2

(The bathroom.)

(The other side of the door)

(VIRGINIA sits in the wheelchair and cries. She muffles the sound with a small towel over her mouth.)

GLENN: *(O S)* You okay in there, Virginia?
(Silence)
Virginia?

VIRGINIA: I'm fine. Thank you.

GLENN: *(O S)* Are you sure?

VIRGINIA: Yes, yes. Thank you…I'm just a little tired.

GLENN: *(O S)* Of course it's going to take time. To feel normal. To feel yourself again. The doctor said it will all take a long time.

VIRGINIA: Yes.

GLENN: *(O S)* No need to rush, right?

VIRGINIA: Yes.

(Silence)

GLENN: *(O S)* I'm here if you need anything.

VIRGINIA: I appreciate that, Glenn.

(Silence)

GLENN: *(O S)* Just yell, okay?
(Silence)
Okay?

VIRGINIA: Yes.
(She stifles another sob.)
(Wipes her eyes)
(She is still crying as she tries to push herself up, using all her strength.)
(She is trying to look in the mirror.)

Scene 3

(GLENN's apartment)

(Morning)

(GLENN pushes VIRGINIA away from the rest room, toward the table.)

(The T V is on. "Good Morning, America" plays loud. They are doing a story on a woman with 19 kids. She is cheerful, happy. [All the girls have long, braided hair and wear long, modest dresses.])

(GLENN keeps his eyes on the T V as he parks VIRGINIA at the table in front of a plate of food.)

(He continues to watch the T V as he refills the coffee cups.)

GLENN: Is this breakfast okay?

VIRGINIA: I'm sorry?

GLENN: Breakfast?

VIRGINIA: I'm sorry, but I can't, I can't hear you.

(GLENN grabs a remote and turns down the T V.)

GLENN: Is the breakfast okay?

VIRGINIA: It looks delicious. Thank you.

GLENN: I didn't know what to make you.

VIRGINIA: This is just right.

GLENN: I normally just have a bowl of bran cereal, but I thought maybe that's a little too dull for your first morning home.

VIRGINIA: Thank you.

GLENN: I guess I should have got some champagne. We could have had mimosas. You like those, I remember.

VIRGINIA: This is perfect. Really.

GLENN: I haven't made an omelette in years.

(VIRGINIA *tastes it.*)

VIRGINIA: You're a good cook.

GLENN: I do alright. I guess it's not rocket science, is it?

VIRGINIA: I guess not.

GLENN: I used to have friends over for dinner parties, cook big gourmet meals, drink lots of expensive wine.

VIRGINIA: Really?

GLENN: In my old house.

VIRGINIA: I see.

GLENN: I'm sorry you never got to see it. I think you would have liked it there. Nice suburb. Big yard. Garden.

VIRGINIA: I'm sorry you had to sell it.

GLENN: That's life.
(He smiles.)
You can't have everything. And you probably don't need it if you got it all anyway... It's just a state of mind. Happiness.

VIRGINIA: Yes. Maybe.

GLENN: I do miss my dogs. But, I'm sure it's good to be in the city. Closer to the hospital. More senior activities.

(The T V pulls GLENN's *attention. A commercial for laundry detergent comes on. A happy housewife tackling tough stains, with fresh scents)*

GLENN: That really does smell fresh.

VIRGINIA: What?

GLENN: That detergent. I use it.

(Silence)

VIRGINIA: Do you watch T V every morning?

GLENN: Pretty much. I like the news. Were at war, you know?

VIRGINIA: Yes. I heard. Are there protests?

GLENN: No. Not really.

VIRGINIA: Why not?

(The T V catches GLENN's *eye again.)*

GLENN: Sometimes I watch the stock report. Though I don't know what I'm watching for anymore. Habit, I guess.
(Silence)
You want me to turn it off?

VIRGINIA: I don't want to interrupt your routine.

GLENN: That's okay.

*(*GLENN *is already pulled into another commercial. A woman cleans her toilet bowl.)*

VIRGINIA: I'm just not…not quite used to the, the scale of it. It's very bright.

GLENN: That's the high definition.

VIRGINIA: I see.

GLENN: We don't have to have it on. It's just commercials right now anyway.

(Another commercial comes on of a woman cleaning her floor as GLENN *turns off the T V. The room seems suddenly empty, too quiet. A void)*

(Long silence)

*(*GLENN *tries to eat his breakfast.)*

GLENN: You sleep okay last night?

VIRGINIA: Well—

GLENN: I laid awake all night. Which isn't surprising really. I mean, it has been forty years since we've slept in the same bed. And honestly, I think I was afraid to sleep because I was afraid that you were going to go to sleep and not wake up.
(He smiles.)
Did you feel me watching you?

VIRGINIA: Yes. Actually.

GLENN: I'm sorry. I couldn't help it. Checking on you every five minutes.

VIRGINIA: Two minutes.

GLENN: What?

VIRGINIA: It felt like you were checking on me every two minutes.

GLENN: Could have been.
(Silence)
It was nice to hold you.

VIRGINIA: Yes.

(Silence)

VIRGINIA: But I kept you awake. Maybe I should sleep out here.

GLENN: No, no. Don't be silly. The couch is too uncomfortable to sleep on. We'll get used to it. It just takes time. No need to rush. I'll take a sleeping pill tonight.

(A knock on the door)

GLENN: I'll get that.
(He goes to the door and opens it.)

(ALMA enters. [She too is older, but has had several very noticeable face-lifts.])

ALMA: Where is she?

GLENN: Alma—

ALMA: I'm so sorry I couldn't get here earlier, but I was away on a retreat and I really couldn't leave.

GLENN: Retreat?

ALMA: Where is she?

GLENN: What kind of retreat?

(ALMA quickly glances at GLENN.)

GLENN: Oh.

(ALMA sees VIRGINIA.)

VIRGINIA: Hi Alma.

ALMA: Do you know how long I've been waiting to hear that? Oh, my goodness, look at you. Look at you. Awake and talking. Glenn, look at her.

GLENN: It's a miracle, isn't it?

ALMA: My goodness.

VIRGINIA: I'm happy to see you.

ALMA: I told Glenn to let them pull the plug on you for years, Virginia. Honestly. I did. I just didn't see the point. I didn't think you were in there anymore. I didn't. But look at you now.

VIRGINIA: I'm here.

ALMA: I wish Mother and Dad could have lived to see you again. And my sweet Jason.

VIRGINIA: Yes. And Tracy. I'd like to see Tracy.

ALMA: Well, no need to bring us all down with that right now. Look at you.

GLENN: Have a seat.

ALMA: No, no, I can't. I'm too excited. There's just so much to catch up on. Right, Glenn?

GLENN: I said the same thing. Where do we begin?

ALMA: Gosh.

VIRGINIA: What happened to your face?

(Silence)

ALMA: What do you mean?

VIRGINIA: You look different.

ALMA: Of course I look different, you haven't seen me in a million years—

VIRGINIA: But it's now how I remember how you used to look. Your eyes are, your mouth—

ALMA: A lot of things may not look how you remembered them. Or they've changed. It's been a long time.

VIRGINIA: Yes, but—

ALMA: And your brain is probably blurry anyway, don't you think? Not being used all that time?

VIRGINIA: No. It's clear.

(Silence)

ALMA: I just don't know where to begin. Do you, Glenn?

GLENN: No.

ALMA: You wouldn't recognize John either. He's fifty pounds heaver. He looks just like his dad now.

GLENN: But he still acts like he's twenty.

ALMA: He likes to think he still looks that way too. Please. As if. Wouldn't we all.

GLENN: I'd like to have my hair.

(Silence)

ALMA: So, Virginia. Tell us. What was it like?

VIRGINIA: What?

ALMA: Being in that coma.

VIRGINIA: Oh. Well—

ALMA: Did you ask her that already, Glenn?

GLENN: No.

ALMA: Why not?

GLENN: I don't know. I just figured she'd talk about when she was ready—

ALMA: Men. Typical.

GLENN: What?

ALMA: Never ask about the elephant in the room.

GLENN: Is that the elephant?

ALMA: I just can't imagine it. I really can't.

VIRGINIA: Well—

ALMA: Was it scary?

VIRGINIA: No—

ALMA: Oh, Glenn, can I have a cup of coffee? I rushed over here this morning and didn't get the chance to have a second cup. I'm barely awake.

GLENN: Sure.

(He exits to get her the coffee.)

ALMA: I just can't imagine. I've had a couple of necessary medical procedures in the last few years— nothing to worry about, thank god—and they put me under anesthesia, and every time, I thought about you, Virginia. I really did. I wondered if I might feel like you were feeling.

VIRGINIA: How'd you feel?

ALMA: Nothing. I don't remember a thing. A complete blank. It was just lost time. Never to be found.

VIRGINIA: Huh.

ALMA: Do you remember anything?

VIRGINIA: Everything.

ALMA: Really? Like what?

VIRGINIA: It's, it's hard to explain, in words. There are so many images and feelings—

ALMA: And there you were, stuck. Like a fossil. No where to go. I just can't imagine what I'd do.

VIRGINIA: Well—

ALMA: But you know, I've never had as good an imagination as you do. I'd probably go crazy or something. Wake up and ask the doctors to shoot me. Like a horse. Which they say is the most humane, but I don't know. A gun is a gun, right? It can't feel like a kiss.

(GLENN *enters with coffee.*)

ALMA: It is just so good to see you. Isn't it Glenn?

GLENN: It's a miracle really.

ALMA: I know. And I don't believe in miracles anymore. I gave up on them.

GLENN: I remember that.

ALMA: I had to. I realized I was just wasting my life. Waiting for the skies to part.

(GLENN *hands* ALMA *coffee.*)

ALMA: And yet, here you are, Virginia. It's really you, right?

VIRGINIA: I think so.

ALMA: And I am forced to ask myself what I believe. Which is probably good for me. To be tested. In positive ways.

VIRGINIA: Yes.

GLENN: Sure.

ALMA: Lord knows I've had my share of the other. When the miracle never came. Day after day.

(GLENN *refills* VIRGINIA's *cup.*)

GLENN: Virginia takes cream in her coffee now.

ALMA: Really?

GLENN: I just assumed everything would be the same.

(VIRGINIA *smiles.*)

VIRGINIA: I've changed. We've all changed—

ALMA: How? You were just laying there.

VIRGINIA: Yes, but my mind was working—

ALMA: I really would have gone crazy. I don't know how you did it. Like a bird stuck in it's own egg. Did you wake up craving anything?

VIRGINIA: What do you mean?

ALMA: Food.

VIRGINIA: Oh. Not really. No—

ALMA: I might have wanted a cheeseburger or something. What about you, Glenn? What do you think you would have wanted to eat?

GLENN: Prime rib.

ALMA: I could have guessed that. Every birthday, he's got to have prime rib. Your husband is a man of habits, Virginia.

VIRGINIA: I don't really eat meat now.

GLENN: You don't?

ALMA: Why not?

VIRGINIA: I told you, things have changed. There are a lot of things that may surprise you about me now.

ALMA: Like what?

GLENN: Of course we don't want to move too fast with any big changes. The doctor said not to rush anything.

ALMA: Of course. You don't want to hurt anything, Virginia.

GLENN: She still has a lot of physical therapy.

ALMA: You're basically like a child, aren't you? You have to relearn everything. I don't know if I could do it.
(*She eats a cookie.*)
What are these? They taste like sawdust.

GLENN: I have to make some adjustments to make this place more Virginia friendly.

ALMA: That's a good idea. Build some ramps or something?
(*About the cookies*)
Are they fat free?

GLENN: Lower the cabinets. Put in a different shower. Yes, they're fat free—

ALMA: (*Still eating*) They're awful—

GLENN: Simple things, you know, but necessary. You don't have to eat them.

VIRGINIA: I don't want you to go to all that trouble, Glenn.

GLENN: It's no trouble.

VIRGINIA: I don't want to be an imposition.

ALMA: He likes to do it. Trust me. He put it in a whole new shelving unit in our garage in two days. He's good with a hammer. Unlike John. He refuses to touch a tool. (Or me, for that matter.)
(She takes another cookie.)

ALMA: These are literally like eating hair.

GLENN: Am I forcing you?

VIRGINIA: Eventually, I'd like to try living alone.

(Silence)

ALMA: That's impossible.

VIRGINIA: Why?

ALMA: Who's going to take care of you?

VIRGINIA: I will.

GLENN: That's not really the plan I had worked out in my head.

ALMA: I don't think you're being realistic.

VIRGINIA: Why not?

ALMA: You've been a vegetable for forty years. For starters.

VIRGINIA: No I haven't—

ALMA: What do you call it?

VIRGINIA: I don't call it anything—

ALMA: And do you know what the medical bills have been for your care? ...Do you have any idea? Glenn went broke keeping you alive.

VIRGINIA: I'm sorry—

ALMA: Every single penny—

VIRGINIA: I never would have wanted him to do that—

ALMA: This is the thanks he gets?

VIRGINIA: Maybe this would be freeing for him. He wouldn't have to worry about me anymore. Can we open a window?

ALMA: Are you kidding? You've become his life's work. He has nothing outside of you.

GLENN: Alma.

ALMA: What?

GLENN: I wouldn't say "nothing". I do have hobbies. I have friends.

(ALMA *rolls her eyes.*)

GLENN: Don't make me sound pathetic. I have hobbies. Interests. I went sailing last year.

ALMA: Big whoop.

GLENN: It was to me.
(*He begins to clear the dishes.*)

ALMA: All those women you could have had? A family? What about that woman who died in the Towers—

GLENN: Please, Alma.

ALMA: This is just a terrible, ridiculous idea. Horrible, Virginia.
(*She holds her face.*)
I can't get upset. It's not good for me right now.
(*She keeps holding her face.*)
I was looking forward to a happy reunion.

VIRGINIA: I'm not trying to spoil anything.

ALMA: But you are—

VIRGINIA: I'm trying to free Glenn of the burden of taking care of me— Can we open a window?

ALMA: Do you know expensive it is to live, at this age, in an apartment by yourself?

VIRGINIA: Can we open a window, please?

GLENN: I can't. Remember?

ALMA: You have no income. You have no social security. You have no life, Virginia.

VIRGINIA: I could really use some air.

GLENN: Alma, please.

ALMA: I just want you to be realistic. You're not a young woman anymore. There are very few options available for older women. Especially older women with no money. You're lucky you have a home here with Glenn. These are hard times. People have to make sacrifices.

VIRGINIA: I've made quite a few sacrifices—

ALMA: Watch the news, Virginia. Read the paper. You'll see. (Oh my face is killing me.)

VIRGINIA: Yes, but I see great things. So many woman are now doctors and lawyers. Who run businesses. A woman is Secretary of State. Seems there are a lot of great opportunities—

ALMA: You're not one of those people.

GLENN: I'm going to wash the dishes.
(He exits with the dishes.)

ALMA: I can't believe you.

VIRGINIA: I really don't want to hurt anyone's feelings. I just want the option to live independently—

ALMA: What do you have in mind? A career in modeling?

VIRGINIA: I don't know.

ALMA: You can't even walk.

VIRGINIA: I need some air.

ALMA: That is a saint in there. You married a saint.

VIRGINIA: Please take me outside, Alma.

ALMA: No.

VIRGINIA: I need some air. I feel like I'm going to—

ALMA: You want to live alone, but you can't even take yourself outside?

VIRGINIA: Alma. Please.
(Silence)
Please.

(ALMA grabs the back of the wheel chair, rather brusquely.)

ALMA: Glenn, I'm taking Virginia outside.

(GLENN enters with a dish towel.)

GLENN: What?

ALMA: I'm taking Virginia outside. She wants some air.

GLENN: You feeling alright?

VIRGINIA: Just want to get outside for a bit.

GLENN: Oh. Okay then. Well. Be careful.

(ALMA pushes VIRGINIA out the door.)

(GLENN looks at the door. His humble apartment)

Scene 4

(Outside)
(ALMA angrily pushes VIRGINIA.)
(Silence)
(Finally:)

VIRGINIA: Are you trying to push me out of this thing?
(Silence)
Or just looking for a cliff.

ALMA: Why, do you see one?

(Silence)

VIRGINIA: A lot has changed, Alma. I keep trying to—

ALMA: But I see some things never change… You still
think you deserve more than everyone else. You're
never satisfied.

VIRGINIA: I want to experience everything I can—

ALMA: Why? What makes you so special, huh?

*(VIRGINIA grabs the wheels. Stopping the wheel chair.
Throwing both ALMA and VIRGINIA off balance.)*

ALMA: Careful! Jesus—

VIRGINIA: I have spent the majority of my life in a
hospital bed. I'm just getting started again. Alive.
Why would you want me to lower my hopes, my
expectations?

ALMA: For your own good.

VIRGINIA: What good can that do me? Or anyone?

ALMA: What harm can it do you?

VIRGINIA: Talk about not changing, Alma. If there's a
glass ceiling, you are one of the people on top, holding
it down, making sure it stays there.

ALMA: That's not true. Why would I do that?

VIRGINIA: I don't know. I really don't.

(Silence)

ALMA: I told you, I just don't think you're being
realistic.

VIRGINIA: It feels like you're trying to keep me in the coma.

ALMA: I would never do that.

VIRGINIA: Maybe I'm easier for you that way.

ALMA: That wasn't easy for anyone. I promise you.

(Silence)

VIRGINIA: If you only knew how hard it was to wake, and come back here. It was the hardest thing I've ever done, coming back to this world, this body…and one of the reasons I came back, was for you.

ALMA: Don't lay this on me.

VIRGINIA: I'm not laying it on you…. I'm just saying I felt I needed to come see you again.

ALMA: Why?

VIRGINIA: You're my sister. I wanted to help you—

ALMA: I don't want you putting all this boloney on me. I was doing fine without you. Frankly.

VIRGINIA: Okay.

ALMA: And poor Glenn.

VIRGINIA: Why?

ALMA: He's a hopeless romantic that man, and he gets nothing from you… You've shattered his fairy tale, Virginia.

VIRGINIA: You're not worth coming back for? Life isn't worth coming back for?

ALMA: I don't think Sleeping Beauty or Snow White were ever kissed by their sisters, or woke up to announce they want to live alone.

VIRGINIA: Maybe none of their sisters had their only son killed at war.

(Silence)

Or were estranged from their only daughter.
(Silence)
Or never left an unhappy marriage.
(Silence)
Or just had a face lift. You are a beautiful woman—

ALMA: What does that have to do with anything?
(She touches her face.)
You're judging me.

VIRGINIA: I'm not.

ALMA: You wake up just to judge me? Is that it?

VIRGINIA: No. What, we can't speak honestly to each other.

ALMA: No.

VIRGINIA: Why not?

ALMA: You think I need that? Listing off my, my life like you pity me.

VIRGINIA: That's not what I meant—

ALMA: Look at you? What do you have?

(Silence)

You're the one in need of pity. Your whole life, wasted. It's not my fault.

(Silence)

VIRGINIA: I'm sorry.
(Silence)
My life wasn't wasted. Was it?

(Silence)

ALMA: I don't like those kind of questions, Virginia. I don't know what the purpose is of asking them... Do we ever really want the answers? Really?

VIRGINIA: Yes.

ALMA: And then what? Will we be happier? Sleep
better? ...I think you start digging deeper in some
places, and you just get stuck digging. I don't see the
point.

VIRGINIA: We're different people.

ALMA: What's wrong with the surface? It's so clean and
simple. You see what's on it. You can glide on by. It's
harmless. I don't know why people keep trying to pull
me off it. All my life...Jason...John... You...George...
Mother...Dad...Tracy.

VIRGINIA: What happened with her, Alma?

ALMA: Don't start digging.

VIRGINIA: What happened?

ALMA: You'd have to ask her.

VIRGINIA: Does she know about me? That I'm awake
and—

ALMA: Her father sent her a letter. Or email. I don't
remember.

VIRGINIA: I'd like to see her—

ALMA: Mother and Dad really wanted to see you again.
They wanted me to tell you that...They tried to hang
on as long as they could... They really did. Mother
was down to eighty pounds. She looked like little bald
bird... And then Dad just kind of faded away. He
didn't know what to do anymore...he was no longer
the man of the house, he was just alone and drunk...
his wife and favorite children stolen from him...and
looking at me just made him angry...I never wanted to
be an only child...I was no good at it.
(Silence)
I'd just like some peace for awhile. I just never seem to
be able to get any peace. My mind's racing all the time.
All day. All night. I wake up exhausted. I don't want

to get out of bed… It never seems to end. The anger. It just never seems to end, Virginia. I never wanted any of this…I just want to glide by.

(She holds her face.)

I don't want to get upset.

(She keeps holding her face.)

Maybe you had it better than any of us…some days, I was so envious of you…I wished I could switch places with you…just stay in bed forever…just sleep it all away.

(She keeps holding her face.)

I don't want to get upset.

Scene 5

(GLENN's apartment)

(GLENN has fallen asleep in front of the television.)

(SUSAN pushes VIRGINIA through the door.)

VIRGINIA: I like the fashion.

SUSAN: It's rags. Nothing but rags and high boots. I feel like I'm surrounded by Hobbits.

(The T V catches their eyes. Several things barrage the screen: A blond reality star [Heidi Montag?] talks about her surgery.)

VIRGINIA: I just can't get used to the size of that T V.

(t's an entertainment news show. [Extra, Entertainment Tonight.])

SUSAN: That's the young woman who had all that plastic surgery. Twenty-three years old. She was under for ten hours. Had ten surgeries in one day. She had a second nose job, second boob job because she wanted bigger boobs—I think she had double Ds put in, they wouldn't put in any bigger—she had her chin shaved

off, cheek implants, butt implants, they carved her back
to make it look more sexy…
(She thinks.)
She had an eye lift, botox, had her ears pinned back,
and…let's see, how many is that?

VIRGINIA: Nine—

SUSAN: Oh, and liposuction. Liposuction on her legs.

VIRGINIA: What's that?

SUSAN: Sucks the fat out.

VIRGINIA: With what?

SUSAN: A hose.

*(SUSAN and VIRGINIA look at the T V as they show pictures
of her bruised, bandaged face, coming out of surgery.)*

SUSAN: If my daughter ever talked to me about doing
something that hateful to her beautiful face, I'd beat
her myself. It's a lot cheaper. And she will still look like
herself when it heals, and not some stranger.

(VIRGINIA keeps watching.)

VIRGINIA: What happened?

SUSAN: I told you. She had surgery. I hear she regrets it
now—

VIRGINIA: No, I mean, what happened.

SUSAN: To what?

VIRGINIA: Is this expected? Is this normal?

SUSAN: It's not expected. But it's normal in some
circles. You don't like your body, your face, you
change it.

VIRGINIA: But—

SUSAN: You gotta look young and thin, Virginia. You
gotta be sexy.

VIRGINIA: Sexy.

SUSAN: Young, thin, and sexy. Yep. All the time. Hell. Look at me. I'm wearing a spanxs right now.

VIRGINIA: What's that?

(SUSAN lifts up her shirt.)

SUSAN: Holds my jiggle in.

(A commercial comes on for Viagra.)

(GLENN wakes.)

VIRGINIA: Erectile disfunction? Is that what they just said?

GLENN: Helps a man get it an erection. (It's wonderful.)

SUSAN: I bet watching T V with you is a trip, Virginia. I bet you feel like you fell down a rabbit hole. It's a whole new world, isn't it.

VIRGINIA: That computer internet sure is something.

SUSAN: Yeah.

VIRGINIA: Talk about a rabbit hole.

GLENN: I've been trying to explain it to her.

SUSAN: Nice to see you, Glenn. How are you?

GLENN: Oh, getting by. You?

SUSAN: Virginia is making great progress. Pretty soon she'll be running laps around you.

GLENN: No need to rush.

SUSAN: Afraid she'll outrun you?

GLENN: She wants to live alone. When she's able.

SUSAN: I heard.

GLENN: Her sister and I think it's a bad idea, don't you? I want her to hear it from a medical professional. Tell her.

(GLENN *turns off the T V.*)

GLENN: Tell her.

SUSAN: Well, if you want my opinion, it didn't make any sense that you kept her alive. Everyone was telling you, you were crazy. "Let her go. Let her go." I heard the doctors. I heard her sister…But you didn't listen. You wanted to keep her alive.

GLENN: Yes, but—

SUSAN: You believed her mind was working. That she would someday wake up.

GLENN: Yes, but—

SUSAN: Then, I guess you have to believe that her mind is still working, and that she can make decisions for herself.

GLENN: But I believed she would wake up to be with me.

SUSAN: That's not her fault.

GLENN: She's my wife.

SUSAN: So she owes you something?

(Silence)

GLENN: It makes no economic or common sense for her to believe that at sixty-six, with no skills, and no income, she can survive on her own. Especially when I am perfectly happy and willing to support and take care of her. I just don't see what's wrong with that. I'm her husband. I've waited, and waited, and waited…I didn't abandon her…I didn't abandon her—

SUSAN: I know—

GLENN: Why would she abandon me now?

VIRGINIA: What does everyone still speak about me in the third person? I'm right here.

GLENN: Can't we just quietly live the last part of our lives together? While we have it? Is that too much to ask?

SUSAN: A lot of patients and families think they can just start up where the left off. The recovery isn't just physical—

GLENN: But they should be willing to try. I think they should be willing to try. Out of respect.

SUSAN: For what?

GLENN: For all the years. Years and years.

SUSAN: And money?

GLENN: I didn't say that, Susan.
(Silence)
I didn't say that, Virginia.
(Silence)
If you want to move out, do it. I can't stop you. But I'm not helping you.

VIRGINIA: Glenn. I'm not trying to hurt you. Couldn't this be good for you too?

(Silence)

SUSAN: Well. Okay then. This has been a lovely visit. I need to get home. My boyfriend is cooking dinner.

GLENN: I thought you were married.

SUSAN: My husband and I got a divorce.

GLENN: Oh. I'm sorry to hear that.

SUSAN: I'm not. Best decision I ever made.

GLENN: I see.

(Silence)

SUSAN: This isn't an easy transition for anybody, the patients, the families, the caretakers. It's traumatic and confusing. I can put you in touch with some counselling services, if you're interested...I'll call you next week, Virginia.

VIRGINIA: Thank you for a lovely afternoon, Susan.

SUSAN: You're welcome.

VIRGINIA: Soon I'll be walking beside you.

SUSAN: I look forward to that.
(She exits.)

(GLENN turns the T V back on. The audiences dances with Ellen Degeneres on her talk show.)

VIRGINIA: Do you resent me?
(Silence)
Glenn?

GLENN: No.

VIRGINIA: Really?

GLENN: No.

VIRGINIA: Please turn the T V off. So we can talk.
(Silence)
Glenn please.

(GLENN turns it off.)

(Silence)

VIRGINIA: Susan told me I almost died three times.

GLENN: Yes.

VIRGINIA: Why did you keep me alive?

GLENN: I felt it was the right thing to do.

VIRGINIA: For you, or for me.

GLENN: For you.

VIRGINIA: Why?

GLENN: I love you.

VIRGINIA: Am I the same person you married?

GLENN: Does it matter?

VIRGINIA: Yes.

(Silence)

I know you had other women…I had plenty of men.

GLENN: What—

VIRGINIA: In my mind.

(GLENN just looks at VIRGINIA. Not sure how to respond to that)

VIRGINIA: I had some of the best years of my life, or what I thought was my life, and sadly, you weren't part of them. I know you had wonderful experiences that I wasn't part of, didn't you?

GLENN: Of course.

VIRGINIA: Our marriage as we knew it, ended a long time ago. We were two people who took a vow to each other when we were kids, and then one day everything changed… We're different people now, aren't we?

GLENN: Does it matter?

VIRGINIA: Yes. It does.

(Silence)

I saw my reflection over and over again today, in every shop window on the street, and I kept thinking there's some old woman in a wheelchair following us. Several times I almost said something to Susan to see if she'd hurry it up a bit and lose that geezer behind us, only to realize that the old geezer following us, was me… And all those men who passed by, who I looked straight at and smiled, never even made eye contact with me. Not one. I was invisible. Totally invisible. I used to turn heads. I used to be watched…I couldn't walk down the street without a man looking at me… Now, I'm lucky if a man holds the door open for the grandma in the wheelchair…okay. That's the deal. I'll accept that…

But when it's just me, and I take a closer look at my face now, I see someone I'd like to get to know. I see a face of someone new, and I want to experience who she is. I can't be the person, the wife you remember me to be. I appreciate that you kept me alive, Glenn, I do, but honestly, I'd have been just as grateful if you had let me go. I could be happy in either world, dead or alive… But since you decided I would stay in this world, and I decided to try and return fully, body and breath…as painful as it's been…please let me decide what my fate will be now, and who and what I will be with my time left.

(Silence)

I want the same for you. You could do so much still—

GLENN: You think divorce and living alone is the answer? You think that is the key to happiness? Freedom?

VIRGINIA: No. No, not necessarily—

GLENN: I know what it's like, Virginia. It's lonely and full of regret. It's a half-life. People are meant to live together. Life is meant be shared. We are built for companionship.

VIRGINIA: Glenn—

GLENN: I've missed you so much.

(Silence)

VIRGINIA: I'm right here.

GLENN: Why did you wake up?

VIRGINIA: For Alma.

(Silence)

And I think I have something more to do with my life. I want to find out.

GLENN: I guess that settles it.

VIRGINIA: What?

GLENN: I've been a fool.

Scene 6

(Morning)

*(*VIRGINIA *sits by the window.)*

*(*GLENN *sits at his computer.)*

(Occasionally she looks over at him.)

(When she is not looking, GLENN *looks at her.)*

VIRGINIA: It's a nice day outside. Blue sky.

*(*GLENN *keeps working on his computer.)*

VIRGINIA: Beautiful.

(She gives up, and keeps her eyes out the window.)

*(*GLENN *does the same, and keeps his eyes on the computer.)*

Scene 7

(Night)

*(*VIRGINIA *wheels into the room and sits in the dark.)*

VIRGINIA: George?

(Silence)

VIRGINIA: George? ...George?

*(*VIRGINIA *finally turns on a light.)*

(She picks up a book from a table. Tries to read, but isn't interested)

(She wheels over to the window, looks out.)

(Unsure of what to do next, she looks around the room.)

(She turns on the television. A news story about the growing restrictions on contraception and abortion in America, state by state.)

(She turns off the T V. Sits quietly for a moment, shaking her head)

(She wheels over to the computer.)

(She moves the mouse and the screen lights up, bright. It's just been sleeping.)

(She clicks the mouse. Slowly types)

(The screen transforms. She clicks the mouse again, and the screen changes.)

(She is entranced.)

Scene 8

(Months later)

(GLENN's apartment.)

(Afternoon)

(VIRGINIA stands by the window. She is now using a walker.)

(She watches and watches out the window.)

(Waves to someone outside)

(Straightens herself up)

(Watches out the window)

(GLENN enters with groceries.)

(Silence)

GLENN: I got the cheese you asked for.

VIRGINIA: Thank you.

GLENN: I used to eat that all the time. When I lived in my old house.

VIRGINIA: Really.

GLENN: I was a gourmet.

VIRGINIA: You still could be.

GLENN: It upsets my stomach.

(VIRGINIA *returns her attention to the window.*)

GLENN: You've been spending a lot of time at that window.

VIRGINIA: I like the view.

(*Silence*)

GLENN: We can't keep on like this, Virginia.

VIRGINIA: Then talk to me.
(*She waves out the window.*)
There's Alma.
(*She uses her walker to walk across the room to the door.*)

GLENN: I'll let her in—

VIRGINIA: No, no. Please. Let me.
(*She makes it to the door, and proudly opens it. Waits*)

ALMA: What?

VIRGINIA: I'm standing.

ALMA: I had to park three blocks away. What do you have to drink?

VIRGINIA: I was thinking we could go downtown. Just you and me.

ALMA: And do what?

VIRGINIA: Enjoy the weather.

GLENN: Get out of this apartment.

ALMA: I just got here.

VIRGINIA: We can sit outside. At a cafe. Susan told me about a nice little French place—

ALMA: We can sit here.

VIRGINIA: Please. It's a nice day.

(Silence)

GLENN: I have some things I need to do anyway.

ALMA: Like what?

GLENN: Work.

ALMA: You're retired.

GLENN: I still have a few clients.

ALMA: Who?

GLENN: You wouldn't know them.

ALMA: How do you know?

GLENN: If Virginia needs to get out of here, just take her Alma. We don't need to go back and forth like this.

ALMA: It's called conversation.

GLENN: It's called badgering.

ALMA: Have you been talking to John?

VIRGINIA: I'll get my purse. My wheelchair's by the door.

ALMA: I thought you were using that walker.

VIRGINIA: I'm just beginning—

ALMA: I don't know if that wheelchair will fit in my car.

GLENN: It'll fit.

ALMA: I'm not sure I'm strong enough to put it in there—

GLENN: I'll do it.

(VIRGINIA sits in the wheelchair.)

ALMA: I'm a terrible driver. John says I'm not safe on the road.

VIRGINIA: I'll take my chances.

Scene 9

(Outdoor cafe)

*(*ALMA *and* VIRGINIA *sit quietly, watching people go by, drinking coffee.)*

VIRGINIA: What a beautiful day. The sun feels good, doesn't it?

ALMA: It's bad for the skin.

(Silence)

VIRGINIA: I don't think I've ever seen anyone take that long to parallel park. I'm still a little sea sick. How about you?

ALMA: I got you here, didn't I?

VIRGINIA: It was touch and go there for awhile.
(She tries to smile at her, lighten her mood.)
But I'm happy to be here. Thank you.

ALMA: You're welcome.

(Silence)

VIRGINIA: So many flowers in bloom. The cherry blossoms are lovely, aren't they?

ALMA: Yes.

VIRGINIA: Why don't you come see me?

ALMA: What do you mean? I'm here, aren't I?

VIRGINIA: For the first time in months. Are you afraid of me?

ALMA: What would I be afraid of?

VIRGINIA: I don't know. But you avoid me.

ALMA: I don't avoid you. I'm just busy. I do have my own life. A husband. Responsibilities.

VIRGINIA: I know—

ALMA: I can't be running over to you every day,
Virginia.

VIRGINIA: I know—

ALMA: I don't know what you expect.

VIRGINIA: Don't you want to spend time together?

ALMA: Sure.

VIRGINIA: Well, what's the problem?

ALMA: There's no problem.

VIRGINIA: I can see right through you, you know. Even
with that new face.

ALMA: See?

VIRGINIA: What?

ALMA: There it is.

VIRGINIA: What?

ALMA: You have to start picking me apart.

VIRGINIA: I'm just teasing you—

ALMA: Well, I don't like your kind of teasing.

VIRGINIA: I'm sorry.

ALMA: It makes me feel bad.

VIRGINIA: I'm sorry—

ALMA: I get enough of that at home. Thank you very
much.

VIRGINIA: I'm sorry, Alma. I will try to be more tactful
from here on out. If that's why you're avoiding me.

ALMA: I'm not avoiding you.

VIRGINIA: We aren't able talk to each for forty years,
and now we get the chance, and you just have nothing
to say to me?

ALMA: I talked to you. All those years, I talked to you.

But now that *you* can talk, well…I don't know…it's like you're an alien.

VIRGINIA: I'm an alien.

ALMA: I'm not used to you speaking back to me.

VIRGINIA: I see—

ALMA: And I don't like the things you say. Frankly.

VIRGINIA: Okay—

ALMA: It's like we thawed out someone from a horror movie. And you might just eat us alive. Or invade the planet. Who knows what you can do.

(VIRGINIA *laughs.*)

ALMA: Seriously. You make me nervous.

VIRGINIA: You like me better mute and comatose.

ALMA: I got used to you that way. You were a terrific listener.

VIRGINIA: Thank you.

ALMA: I could tell you anything. I miss my confidant.

VIRGINIA: I miss my sister.
(*Silence*)
Dad used to say that whenever you take a trip, or experience something that changed you, no one really wants to hear about it. Remember? He said people aren't really interested in listening to things they haven't felt or known themselves. Don't even try, he said… Now I know what he meant.

ALMA: Yet he used to make us sit through those damn slide shows.

VIRGINIA: But he never talked about the war. And mother never talked about George once he went missing. She just stopped speaking his name.

(*Silence*)

ALMA: Well, if you were a mother, you might understand.

VIRGINIA: Maybe.

ALMA: You should feel lucky you didn't ever have children, Virginia.

VIRGINIA: Maybe. I don't know—

ALMA: All you pour into them, and they can die, leave or reject you in a heartbeat. Everything you've done for them, your entire life sacrificed just for them, means nothing… No one ever told me about that… It can be the biggest scam around, motherhood… Maybe we should order cocktails instead.

VIRGINIA: If you want.

ALMA: See, you're doing it again.

VIRGINIA: What?

ALMA: Slyly peeling me away.

VIRGINIA: I'm just sitting here trying to talk to you.

ALMA: No you're not.

VIRGINIA: I love you, Alma. I just want to talk—

ALMA: Everyone who is supposed to love me in my life is like a fucking buzz saw. All the time. Tearing at me. I'm bloody with love.

(TRACY *JENNINGS enters. Nicely dressed)*

TRACY: You didn't tell me my mother would be here.

VIRGINIA: Oh my goodness. Look at you, Tracy. All grown up and beautiful.

TRACY: Please. I look terrible. I've been in meetings all day.
(*She looks at* ALMA.)
You really should have told me my mother would be—

VIRGINIA: Your mother's here.

ALMA: That's a nice suit. It looks expensive.

TRACY: Thank you. I'm glad you approve.

ALMA: Here we go.

VIRGINIA: Please, have a seat. We were just getting ready to order cocktails.

TRACY: *(To* ALMA*)* You're still drinking?

ALMA: I'll be drinking *a lot* today.

TRACY: Aunt Virginia, I don't know if I can stay—

VIRGINIA: Sit.

TRACY: She's an alcoholic.

VIRGINIA: Sit.

TRACY: This is why we stopped talking—

VIRGINIA: Sit. Please.

*(*TRACY *finally sits, reluctantly.)*

*(*ALMA *adjusts her hair.)*

ALMA: I'm not an alcoholic. I'm a recreational drinker. *(To* VIRGINIA*)*
This was your idea?

VIRGINIA: Yes.

ALMA: See? You're invading.

TRACY: I see you got yet another face lift, Mother.

ALMA: I'm not in the mood.

TRACY: I just don't see why you keep doing that to yourself—

ALMA: I said, I'm not in the mood.

VIRGINIA: Well—

TRACY: You would be so beautiful without them.

*(*ALMA *hears this. Looks at* TRACY*)*

TRACY: It's true. And it's not going to keep Dad from fucking those other women.

ALMA: Is that necessary?

VIRGINIA: What a lovely day. To be together.

ALMA: Did it ever occur to you that it's none of your business what I do with my face? And that what I do might have nothing to do with your father?
(*Silence*)
You know nothing about me.

TRACY: I'm sorry.

ALMA: I need a drink.

TRACY: (*To* VIRGINIA) I'm sorry.

VIRGINIA: Do you have any trouble finding the place?

TRACY: The cab driver knew where it was.

VIRGINIA: Good, good. I'm so happy to see you.

TRACY: You too.

ALMA: Are you still living in that, that, that place, what do you call it…?

TRACY: Los Angeles?

ALMA: Yes.

TRACY: Yes. I'm just in town for a conference.

ALMA: Why would you want to live in that place, Tracy? No one takes anyone seriously from Los Angeles.

TRACY: Then why am I the guest speaker at the conference?

ALMA: What are they selling, surf boards?

(TRACY *takes a deep breath.* VIRGINIA *grabs her hand.*)

VIRGINIA: So nice we get to see each other. A nice family gathering. How fortunate I feel.

ALMA: Where the hell is that waiter?

TRACY: It is really remarkable that you've recovered the way you have, Aunt Virginia.

VIRGINIA: Thank you.

TRACY: How do you feel?

VIRGINIA: A little strange and overwhelmed at times, but overall, good.

TRACY: My ex was a neurologist and I called and told him you had come out of the coma. Even he was shocked—

ALMA: She wouldn't marry him, so he left her.

TRACY: That's not true—

ALMA: You had a chance to get married, and you blew it.

TRACY: Why would I want to get married, after the mockery that I grew up with?

VIRGINIA: Where is that waiter?

TRACY: I wasn't in love with him, Mother, and I left him.

ALMA: If that's what you tell yourself.
(Silence)
And now look at you. Still single. No children.

TRACY: And happy. Which is a lot more than you can say for your own life. A lot more. So zip it, okay. "I'm not in the mood."

ALMA: Is this how you speak to your patients?

VIRGINIA: Maybe we should get some appetizers.

ALMA: You wouldn't speak to your worst enemy the way you speak to me.

TRACY: That's not true.

VIRGINIA: I'm so glad we are all together—

ALMA: For all his faults, at least your brother was sweet to me.

TRACY: Jason was an asshole to you—

ALMA: Don't you dare say that about your brother. He was my son, and I knew he loved me. More than you ever have.

VIRGINIA: Where on earth is that waiter—

TRACY: We all know you loved Jason more than me. So let's not reinvent the past—

ALMA: You have given me nothing but sneers and insults, Tracy. Since you were six months old. I got a sneer before I ever got a smile out of you...And now twelve years of silence. If it weren't for me, you wouldn't be alive, for Christ's sake. And yet you're ashamed I exist.

TRACY: I'm not ashamed—

ALMA: What's the point of having a daughter who hates you? Who finds no value in your very existence, or your choices in life?

TRACY: I don't hate you.

(ALMA *stands.*)

ALMA: What I don't understand is, why it still matters? ...Who I am? ...You're forty-three. Successful. Independent. Plenty of your own money. No husband. No children. You don't clean your own house... You don't cook your own meals... You say you have everything you want... *You have not become me.* In any way. Congratulations, Tracy. You did it!

TRACY: Mom—

ALMA: And I have done my job as mother. I raised a daughter who can take care of herself. A doctor. A

modern woman. Good for me. I did it! Hurray for
me! I fulfilled my promise to the next generation! The
feminist dream! I helped make it happen! Hurray for
me! Hurray for me! ...And what do *I* get? A pat on the
back? A medal?
(She points to TRACY's *face.)*
I get *that* look. (Those are my eyes: same shape, same
color, everything.) Without an ounce of gratitude. Or
pride. Or love.
(She puts some money on the table.)
You can take a taxi home, Virginia.

VIRGINIA: No, Alma. Stay—

TRACY: Mom.

ALMA: Peas in a pod, you two... You say you woke up
for me, Virginia? To help me? Help me do what? ...
Well, don't wait for any thank you's. I don't need you.
If this is love, I don't need love either. I've done fine
without it all these years.
(She grabs her coat off the chair.)
Believe it or not, I like who I am. I realize I'm not who
you both want me to be, and I'm not Sunny Brooke
Farms Holly Go Lightly Jingle Bells of Joy Alma
Jennings, but I like myself. I free you to stop wasting
your time trying to change, and help, and judge,
and *understand* the shadowy depths of this sixty-two
year-old woman, and concentrate on understanding
yourselves.
(She exits.)

(Silence)

VIRGINIA: She's seventy.

TRACY: I thought so.

(Silence)

VIRGINIA: I'm sorry.

TRACY: My relationship with my mother is just something my mother and I have to figure out. Or leave alone.

VIRGINIA: You need to make an effort, Tracy. No matter what. Keep trying.

TRACY: It's not that easy. As you can see—

VIRGINIA: Not for you. For her... You get to be a certain age, and you really need to know that all the years add up to something. There's been some small impact, somewhere, by you being alive... That you've been of value. To someone. Some thing.

(Silence)

TRACY: I came to see you once. When Jason died. I opened the door and saw all the machines they had you hooked up to, and I just couldn't go in. I didn't want to see you that way.

VIRGINIA: I must have looked pretty pathetic.

TRACY: Mother used to cry for hours after visiting you. And drink. It became a ritual.

(Silence)

VIRGINIA: I miss it.

TRACY: What?

VIRGINIA: That place.

TRACY: The coma?

VIRGINIA: I know it's hard for you to imagine, but I was invincible there. Here, I'm...limited.

TRACY: No you're not. Look at you. It's remarkable—

VIRGINIA: A freak and trophy for modern medicine.

TRACY: You're not a freak. But be careful. That's my profession.

VIRGINIA: I'm sure you're doing wonderful things.

TRACY: I hope so.

VIRGINIA: I'm proud of you.

TRACY: Well, being a fertility doctor has just proved to be more fuel for my mother. She can't understand why I won't just "implant" her grandchildren.
(Silence)
Actually, I may end up doing that.
(Silence)
I'm not as happy as I tell her I am.
(Silence)
Maybe I'm afraid my life is actually more empty than hers.
(Silence)
Anyway.
(She smiles.)
Where the hell is that waiter?

Scene 10

(GLENN's apartment)

(Months later)

(The bedroom. Night)

(GLENN begins to help VIRGINIA into the bed. By routine. Silently)

VIRGINIA: I, I can do it. Thank you.
(She pulls her legs up, and onto the bed, and settles in.)

(GLENN climbs into the other side and grabs his glasses and book. Begins to read)

VIRGINIA: That was a very good dinner, Glenn. Thank you.

GLENN: You're welcome.

VIRGINIA: You've really become a good cook. I remember when you wouldn't even go near the kitchen.

(Silence)

VIRGINIA: Remember that?

GLENN: I had to learn, I guess.

VIRGINIA: Yes.

(Silence)

I imagine you had to learn many things you didn't plan on learning.

GLENN: Uh huh.

(Silence)

VIRGINIA: I wonder what happened to the man who threw that beer can into the crowd. Do you ever think about him?

GLENN: No.

VIRGINIA: I do. I wonder if he's still alive. If he thinks about that day. How he changed everything for us. In that instant.

(Silence)

Maybe if that hadn't changed things, something else might have come along.

GLENN: Maybe.

(Silence)

VIRGINIA: I don't think life is really that interested in us, at all. I think it's indifferent. As much as we'd like to think it's got some big plan for us, or we for it, I don't think the plans matter one bit on either side. Plans are just mental exercises between the real events that occur that actually change us. That make us who we are. That transform our history...We cling to the plans, but they're just, just like birds passing, and then

they disappear and you're left with all that sky. You're
still left with all that sky. And what does it mean? How
far does it go? Where will it take you? Who is listening?
(Silence)
Where do all those birds go?

(VIRGINIA smiles at GLENN. He keeps reading.)

GLENN: When are you leaving?

VIRGINIA: Tomorrow.

(Silence)

GLENN: Tracy found you a place then?

VIRGINIA: Well, a friend of a friend of a friend of
hers from college found it. It's government housing.
Subsidized. Near Capitol Hill.

GLENN: I see.

VIRGINIA: Nothing fancy, of course, but it will be mine.

(Silence)

GLENN: You must be happy about that.

VIRGINIA: Yes.

GLENN: Good—

VIRGINIA: But not as happy as I thought I would be.

(GLENN finally puts down the book and takes off his glasses.)

GLENN: It can be kinda rough in that part of town, you
know.

VIRGINIA: I'll be fine.

GLENN: I'm serious. You have to be careful.

VIRGINIA: It's close to many things. Government
offices. I could get involved in something.

GLENN: Doing what?

VIRGINIA: I don't know. Teach. Listen. Volunteer.
There must be some use for an old woman in America,
somewhere. Right?

(Silence)

Right?

GLENN: Of course.

(Silence)

VIRGINIA: I've still got all that sky, Glenn. I need to
figure out where it goes. I'm not done.

GLENN: I know.

(VIRGINIA grabs GLENN's hand.)

VIRGINIA: You've been a wonderful husband. I couldn't
have asked for better. I want you to know that. I
married the right man.

GLENN: You don't have to go.

VIRGINIA: I do.

(Silence)

GLENN: Then what?

(Silence)

VIRGINIA: Well. We'll visit each other. We'll learn how
to talk again. We'll talk on the phone. We'll e-mail.
We'll catch up on the years we've missed together.
We'll tell each other everything we remember before
we forget it.

(Silence)

We'll visit Alma. We'll visit Susan… We'll talk to Tracy
on the phone. We'll make new friends and talk about
them to each other… We'll walk down the streets of
Washington together. We'll visit the Vietnam Memorial
and we'll find George's name. And I will finally say
good-bye to my brother.

(Silence)

And you'll drop me off at my apartment and we'll kiss good night and every time I will say thank you for devoting your life to me when other men might have left years ago…and thank you for respecting my choice to leave you, so that I might figure out my place in this strange, new world.

(Silence)

GLENN: Those sound like plans, Virginia.

VIRGINIA: And I'm clinging to them because I don't know what else to do.

(Silence)

They're all we've got, sweetheart. Sometimes, they're all we've got. Right?

(She kisses him.)

(GLENN *reaches to turn out the light.)*

END OF PLAY